Lyrical Ballads: 1798 and 1800

William Wordsworth; Samuel Taylor Coleridge

GRAPEVINE INDIA

Published by

GRAPEVINE INDIA PUBLISHERS PVT LTD

www.grapevineindia.com
Delhi | Mumbai
email: grapevineindiapublishers@gmail.com

Ordering Information:
Quantity sales: Special discounts are available on quantity
purchases by corporations, associations, and others.
For details, reach out to the publisher.

First published by Grapevine India 2023
Copyright © Grapevine 2023
All rights reserved

THE RIME OF THE ANCYENT MARINERE,
IN SEVEN PARTS.

It is an ancyent Marinere,

And he stoppeth one of three:

"By thy long grey beard and thy glittering eye

Now wherefore stoppest me?

The Bridegroom's doors are open'd wide

And I am next of kin;

The Guests are met, the Feast is set,—

May'st hear the merry din."

But still he holds the wedding-guest—

There was a Ship, quoth he—   10

"Nay, if thou'st got a laughsome tale,

Marinere! come with me."

He holds him with his skinny hand,

Quoth he, there was a Ship—

"Now get thee hence, thou grey-beard Loon!

Or my Staff shall make thee skip."

He holds him with his glittering eye—

The wedding guest stood still

And listens like a three year's child;

The Marinere hath his will.   20

The wedding-guest sate on a stone,

He cannot chuse but hear:

And thus spake on that ancyent man,

The bright-eyed Marinere.

The Ship was cheer'd, the Harbour clear'd—

Merrily did we drop

Below the Kirk,1 below the Hill,

Below the Light-house top.

1 Kirk] The name for a church in northern England and Scotland.

The Sun came up upon the left,

Out of the Sea came he: 30

And he shone bright, and on the right

Went down into the Sea.

Higher and higher every day,

Till over the mast at noon—1

The wedding-guest here beat his breast,

For he heard the loud bassoon.

The Bride hath pac'd into the Hall,

Red as a rose is she;

Nodding their heads before her goes

The merry Minstralsy.2 40

The wedding-guest he beat his breast,

Yet he cannot chuse but hear:

And thus spake on that ancyent Man,

The bright-eyed Marinere.

Listen, Stranger! Storm and Wind,

A Wind and Tempest strong!

For days and weeks it play'd us freaks3—

Like Chaff we drove along.

Listen, Stranger! Mist and Snow,4

And it grew wond'rous cauld: 50

And Ice mast-high came floating by

As green as Emerauld.

And thro' the drifts the snowy clifts

Did send a dismal sheen;5

Higher ... noon] As the ship travels further south, the sun appears higher in the sky each day.

Minstralsy] "Minstrelsy," a group of musicians.

Listen ... freaks] 1800: "But now the Northwind came more fierce,/There came a Tempest strong!/And Southward still for days and weeks." freaks] Tricks.

Listen ... Snow] 1800: "And now there came both Mist and Snow,"

sheen] A gleam, as of something reflecting light.

Ne shapes of men ne1 beasts we ken2—

The Ice was all between.

The Ice was here, the Ice was there,

The Ice was all around:

It crack'd and growl'd, and roar'd and howl'd—

Like noises of a swound.3   60

At length did cross an Albatross,

Thorough the Fog it came;

And an4 it were a Christian Soul,

We hail'd it in God's name.

The Marineres gave it biscuit-worms,

And round and round it flew:

The Ice did split with a Thunder-fit;

The Helmsman steer'd us thro'.

And a good south wind sprung up behind,

The Albatross did follow;   70

And every day for food or play

Came to the Marinere's hollo!

In mist or cloud on mast or shroud

It perch'd for vespers nine,

Whiles all the night thro' fog-smoke white

Glimmer'd the white moon-shine.

"God save thee, ancyent Marinere!

From the fiends that plague thee thus—

Why look'st thou so?"—with my cross bow

I shot the Albatross.   80

Ne ... ne] Neither, nor. 1800: "ne" is changed to "nor" throughout the poem.

ken] Recognize, discover.

Like ... swound] 1800: "A wild and ceaseless sound." swound] Swoon.

an] As if.

II

The Sun came up upon the right,

Out of the Sea came he;

And broad as a weft1 upon the left2

Went down into the Sea.

And the good south wind still blew behind,

But no sweet Bird did follow

Ne any day for food or play

Came to the Marinere's hollo!

And I had done an hellish thing

And it would work 'em woe: 90 For all averr'd, I had kill'd the Bird That made the Breeze to blow.

Ne dim ne red, like God's own head,3 The glorious Sun uprist:4

Then all averr'd, I had kill'd the Bird That brought the fog and mist.

'Twas right, said they, such birds to slay That bring the fog and mist.

The breezes blew, the white foam flew,

The furrow5 follow'd free: 100

We were the first that ever burst

Into that silent Sea.

Down dropt the breeze, the Sails dropt down, 'Twas sad as sad could be And we did speak only to break

The silence of the Sea.

All in a hot and copper sky

The bloody sun at noon,

Right up above the mast did stand,

No bigger than the moon.   110 weft] A streak of cloud or thin layer of mist.

And ... left] 1800: "Still hid in mist; and on the left"

Ne ... head] 1800: "Nor dim nor red, like an Angel's head,"

uprist] Arose; in medieval English, the word also meant "to rise from the dead."

furrow] A trench in the earth made by a plow; here, the track of a vessel on the sea.

Day after day, day after day,

We stuck, ne breath ne motion,

As idle as a painted Ship

Upon a painted Ocean.

Water, water, every where

And all the boards did shrink;

Water, water, every where,

Ne any drop to drink.

The very deeps did rot: O Christ!

That ever this should be!   120

Yea, slimy things did crawl with legs

Upon the slimy Sea.

About, about, in reel and rout

The Death-fires danc'd at night;

The water, like a witch's oils,

Burnt green and blue and white.1

And some in dreams assured were

Of the Spirit2 that plagued us so:

Nine fathom deep he had follow'd us

From the Land of Mist and Snow.   130

And every tongue thro' utter drouth3

Was wither'd at the root;

We could not speak no more than if

We had been choked with soot.

Ah wel-a-day! what evil looks

Had I from old and young;

Instead of the Cross the Albatross

About my neck was hung.

About ... white] Referring to the luminous appearance of the sea caused by dinoflagellates, greenish-white microscopic organisms.

Spirit] The sailors are likely thinking of the Each Uisge or the Kelpie, a malignant water spirit of Scottish mythology. See also line 147 of this poem.

drouth] Thirst.

III

I saw a something in the Sky

No bigger than my fist;1   140

At first it seem'd a little speck

And then it seem'd a mist:

It mov'd and mov'd, and took at last

A certain shape, I wist.2

A speck, a mist, a shape, I wist!

And still it ner'd and ner'd;

And, an it dodg'd a water-sprite,

It plung'd and tack'd and veer'd.

With throat unslack'd, with black lips bak'd

Ne could we laugh, ne wail: 150

Then while thro' drouth all dumb they stood

I bit my arm and suck'd the blood

And cry'd, A sail! a sail!

With throat unslack'd, with black lips bak'd

Agape they hear'd me call:

Gramercy!3 they for joy did grin

And all at once their breath drew in

As they were drinking all.

She doth not tack from side to side—4

Hither to work us weal5   160

I saw ... fist] 1800: "So past a weary time; each throat/Was parch'd, and glaz'd each eye,/When, looking westward, I beheld/A something in the sky." Lines 141–44 then follow in a new stanza.

wist] Thought.

Gramercy!] A shortened form of "God grant mercy on us!"

She ... side—] 1800: "See! See! (I cry'd) she tacks no more!"

weal] Good.

Withouten wind, withouten tide1

She steddies with upright keel.

The western wave was all a flame,

The day was well nigh done!

Almost upon the western wave

Rested the broad bright Sun;

When that strange shape drove suddenly

Betwixt us and the Sun.

And strait the Sun was fleck'd with bars

(Heaven's mother send us grace)   170

As if thro' a dungeon grate he peer'd

With broad and burning face.

Alas! (thought I, and my heart beat loud)

How fast she neres and neres!

Are those her Sails that glance in the Sun

Like restless gossameres?2

Are those her naked ribs, which fleck'd

The sun that did behind them peer?

And are those two all, all the crew,

That woman and her fleshless Pheere?3   180

His bones were black with many a crack,

All black and bare, I ween;4

Jet-black and bare, save where with rust

Of mouldy damps and charnel crust

They're patch'd with purple and green.

Her lips are red, her looks are free,

Her locks are yellow as gold:

Her skin is white as leprosy,

And she is far liker Death than he;

Her flesh makes the still air cold.   190

The naked Hulk alongside came

And the Twain were playing dice;

"The Game is done! I've won, I've won!"

Quoth she, and whistled thrice.

A gust of wind sterte up behind

And whistled thro' his bones;

Thro' the holes of his eyes and the hole of his mouth

Half-whistles and half-groans.

With never a whisper in the Sea

Off darts the Spectre-ship; 200 While clombe above the Eastern bar

The horned Moon, with one bright Star Almost atween the tips.1

One after one by the horned Moon

(Listen, O Stranger! to me)

Each turn'd his face with a ghastly pang And curs'd me with his ee.2

Four times fifty living men,

With never a sigh or groan,

With heavy thump, a lifeless lump 210 They dropp'd down one by one.

Their souls did from their bodies fly,—

They fled to bliss or woe;

And every soul it pass'd me by,

Like the whiz of my Cross-bow.

Withouten ... tide] 1798: "Without a breeze, without a tide"

gossameres] Any sheer cloth; also, filmy cobwebs often seen floating in the air in calm weather.

Are those ... Pheere] 1800: "Are those her Ribs, thro' which the Sun/Did peer, as thro' a grate?/And are those two all, all her crew,/That Woman, and her Mate?" Pheere] variant of "fere," meaning "companion" or "mate."

ween] Believe.

IV

"I fear thee, ancyent Marinere!

I fear thy skinny hand;

And thou art long and lank and brown As is the ribb'd Sea-sand.

I fear thee and thy glittering eye   220

And thy skinny hand so brown—"

Fear not, fear not, thou wedding guest!

This body dropt not down.

Alone, alone, all all alone

Alone on the wide wide Sea;

And Christ would take no pity on

My soul in agony.

The many men so beautiful,

And they all dead did lie!

And a million million slimy things   230

Liv'd on—and so did I.

I look'd upon the rotting Sea,

And drew my eyes away;

I look'd upon the eldritch1 deck,

And there the dead men lay.

I look'd to Heaven, and try'd to pray;

But or ever a prayer had gusht,

A wicked whisper came and made

My heart as dry as dust.

I clos'd my lids and kept them close,   240

Till the balls like pulses beat;

For the sky and the sea, and the sea and the sky

Lay like a load on my weary eye,

And the dead were at my feet.

The cold sweat melted from their limbs,

Ne rot, ne reek did they;

The look with which they look'd on me,

Had never pass'd away.

An orphan's curse would drag to Hell

A spirit from on high: 250

But O! more horrible than that

Is the curse in a dead man's eye!

Seven days, seven nights I saw that curse,

And yet I could not die.

The moving Moon went up the sky

And no where did abide:

Softly she was going up

And a star or two beside—

Her beams bemock'd the sultry main

Like morning frosts yspread;1   260

But where the ship's huge shadow lay,

The charmed water burnt alway

A still and awful red.

Beyond the shadow of the ship

I watch'd the water-snakes:

They mov'd in tracks of shining white;

And when they rear'd, the elfish light

Fell off in hoary flakes.

Within the shadow of the ship

I watch'd their rich attire: 270

Blue, glossy green, and velvet black

They coil'd and swam; and every track

Was a flash of golden fire.

O happy living things! no tongue

Their beauty might declare:

A spring of love gusht from my heart,

And I bless'd them unaware!

Sure my kind saint took pity on me,

And I bless'd them unaware.

The self-same moment I could pray;   280

And from my neck so free

The Albatross fell off, and sank

Like lead into the sea.

1 eldritch] 1800: "ghastly"

The horned ... tips] Presumably a crescent moon rising in the Eastern sky with a bright star, probably Mars or Venus.

ee] Eye.

V

O sleep, it is a gentle thing

Belov'd from pole to pole!

To Mary-queen1 the praise be yeven2

She sent the gentle sleep from heaven

That slid into my soul.

The silly3 buckets on the deck

That had so long remain'd,   290

I dreamt that they were fill'd with dew

And when I awoke it rain'd.

My lips were wet, my throat was cold,

My garments all were dank;

Sure I had drunken in my dreams

And still my body drank.

I mov'd and could not feel my limbs,

I was so light, almost

I thought that I had died in sleep,

And was a blessed Ghost.   300

The roaring wind! it roar'd far off,4

It did not come anear;

But with its sound it shook the sails

That were so thin and sere.

The upper air5 bursts into life,

And a hundred fire-flags6 sheen

To and fro they are hurried about;

And to and fro, and in and out

The stars dance on between.

The coming wind doth roar more loud; 310

The sails do sigh, like sedge:7

The rain pours down from one black cloud And the Moon is at its edge.1

Hark! hark! the thick black cloud is cleft,

And the Moon is at its side:

Like waters shot from some high crag,

The lightning falls with never a jag

A river steep and wide.2

The strong wind reach'd the ship: it roar'd

And dropp'd down, like a stone!3 320

Beneath the lightning and the moon

The dead men gave a groan.

They groan'd, they stirr'd, they all uprose,

Ne spake, ne mov'd their eyes:

And I quak'd to think of my own voice

How frightful it would be!4

1 Like ... yspread] 1800: "Like April hoar-frost spread;"Mary-queen] The Virgin Mary.

yeven] Given.

silly] Plain or rustic.

The roaring ... far off] 1800: "And soon I heard a roaring wind,"

upper air] Upper atmosphere.

fire-flags] Meteoric flames.

sedge] Coarse, rush-like plants found in swamps.

The upper ... edge] The 1800 edition revises these lines into the past tense.

The ... wide] The 1800 edition revises these lines into the past tense.

The ... stone] 1800: "The loud wind never reach'd the Ship,/Yet now the Ship mov'd on!"

And ... be!] 1800: deletes these lines and replaces them with an addi-

tional stanza: "'I fear thee, ancient Mariner!'/Be calm, thou wedding guest!/'Twas not those souls, that fled in pain,/Which to their corses came again,/But a troop of Spirits blest:"

The day-light1 dawn'd—they dropp'd their arms,

And cluster'd round the mast: 340

Sweet sounds rose slowly thro' their mouths

And from their bodies pass'd.

Around, around, flew each sweet sound,

Then darted to the sun:

Slowly the sounds came back again

Now mix'd, now one by one.

Sometimes a dropping from the sky

I heard the Lavrock2 sing;

Sometimes all little birds that are

How they seem'd to fill the sea and air 350 With their sweet jargoning,

And now 'twas like all instruments,

Now like a lonely flute;

And now it is an angel's song

That makes the heavens be mute.

It ceas'd: yet still the sails made on

A pleasant noise till noon,

A noise like of a hidden brook

In the leafy month of June,

That to the sleeping woods all night 360 Singeth a quiet tune.

Listen, O listen, thou Wedding-guest!

"Marinere! thou hast thy will:

For that, which comes out of thine eye, doth make My body and soul to be still."

Never sadder tale was told

To a man of woman born:

Sadder and wiser thou wedding-guest!

Thou'lt rise to morrow morn.

Never sadder tale was heard   370

By a man of woman born:

The Marineres all return'd to work

As silent as beforne.

The Marineres all 'gan pull the ropes,

But look at me they n'old:1

Thought I, I am as thin as air—

They cannot me behold.2

Till noon we silently sail'd on

Yet never a breeze did breathe:

Slowly and smoothly went the ship   380

Mov'd onward from beneath.

Under the keel nine fathom deep

From the land of mist and snow

The spirit slid: and it was He

That made the Ship to go.

The sails at noon left off their tune

And the Ship stood still also.

The sun right up above the mast

Had fix'd her to the ocean:

But in a minute she 'gan stir   390

With a short uneasy motion—

Backwards and forwards half her length

With a short uneasy motion.

Then, like a pawing horse let go,

She made a sudden bound:

It flung the blood into my head,

And I fell into a swound.

How long in that same fit I lay,

I have not to declare;

But ere my living life return'd, 400

I heard and in my soul discern'd

Two voices in the air,

"Is it he?" quoth one, "Is this the man?

By him who died on cross,

With his cruel bow he lay'd full low

The harmless Albatross.

The spirit who 'bideth by himself

In the land of mist and snow,

He lov'd the bird that lov'd the man

Who shot him with his bow." 410

The other was a softer voice,

As soft as honey-dew:

Quoth he, "The man hath penance done,

And penance more will do."

The day-light] 1800: "For when it"

Lavrock] 1800: "Sky-lark"

n'old] An archaic form of "nill," meaning "would not."

Listen ... behold] 1800: lines 362-77 deleted.

VI

FIRST VOICE

"But tell me, tell me! speak again,

Thy soft response renewing—

What makes that ship drive on so fast?

What is the Ocean doing?"

SECOND VOICE

"Still as a Slave before his Lord,

The Ocean hath no blast: 420

His great bright eye most silently

Up to the moon is cast—

If he may know which way to go,

For she guides him smooth or grim.

See, brother, see! how graciously

She looketh down on him."

FIRST VOICE

"But why drives on that ship so fast

Withouten wave or wind?"

SECOND VOICE

"The air is cut away before,

And closes from behind.   430

Fly, brother, fly! more high, more high,

Or we shall be belated:

For slow and slow that ship will go,

When the Marinere's trance is abated."

I woke, and we were sailing on

As in a gentle weather:

'Twas night, calm night, the moon was high;

The dead men stood together.

All stood together on the deck,

For a charnel-dungeon fitter: 440

All fix'd on me their stony eyes

That in the moon did glitter.

The pang, the curse, with which they died,

Had never pass'd away:

I could not draw my een1 from theirs

Ne turn them up to pray.

And in its time the spell was snapt,

And I could move my een:2

I look'd far-forth, but little saw

Of what might else be seen.   450

Like one, that on a lonely road

Doth walk in fear and dread,

And having once turn'd round, walks on

And turns no more his head:

Because he knows, a frightful fiend

Doth close behind him tread.

But soon there breath'd a wind on me,

Ne sound ne motion made:

een] 1800: "eyes"

And in ... een] 1800: "And now this spell was snapt: once more/I view'd the ocean green,"

Its path was not upon the sea

In ripple or in shade.   460

It rais'd my hair, it fann'd my cheek,

Like a meadow-gale of spring—

It mingled strangely with my fears,

Yet it felt like a welcoming.

Swiftly, swiftly flew the ship,

Yet she sail'd softly too:

Sweetly, sweetly blew the breeze—

On me alone it blew.

O dream of joy! is this indeed

The light-house top I see? 470

Is this the Hill? Is this the Kirk?

Is this mine own countrée?

We drifted o'er the Harbour-bar,

And I with sobs did pray—

"O let me be awake, my God!

Or let me sleep alway!"

The harbour-bay was clear as glass,

So smoothly it was strewn!

And on the bay the moon light lay,

And the shadow of the moon. 480

The moonlight bay was white all o'er,

Till rising from the same,

Full many shapes, that shadows were,

Like as of torches came.

A little distance from the prow

Those dark-red shadows were;

But soon I saw that my own flesh

Was red as in a glare.

I turn'd my head in fear and dread,

And by the holy rood,1 490

The bodies had advanc'd, and now

Before the mast they stood.

They lifted up their stiff right arms,

They held them strait and tight;

And each right-arm burnt like a torch,
A torch that's borne upright.
Their stony eye-balls glitter'd on
In the red and smoky light.
I pray'd and turn'd my head away
Forth looking as before. 500
There was no breeze upon the bay,
No wave against the shore.1
The rock shone bright, the kirk no less
That stands above the rock:
The moonlight steep'd in silentness
The steady weathercock.

And the bay was white with silent light,
Till rising from the same
Full many shapes, that shadows were,
In crimson colours came. 510
A little distance from the prow
Those crimson shadows were:
I turn'd my eyes upon the deck—
O Christ! what saw I there?
Each corse lay flat, lifeless and flat;
And by the Holy rood
A man all light, a seraph-man,
On every corse there stood.

This seraph-band, each wav'd his hand:
It was a heavenly sight: 520

They stood as signals to the land,

Each one a lovely light:

This seraph-band, each wav'd his hand, No voice did they impart—

No voice; but O! the silence sank,

Like music on my heart.

Eftsones1 I heard the dash of oars,

I heard the pilot's cheer:

My head was turn'd perforce away

And I saw a boat appear.   530

Then vanish'd all the lovely lights;

The bodies rose anew:

With silent pace, each to his place,

Came back the ghastly crew.

The wind, that shade nor motion made,

On me alone it blew.2

The pilot, and the pilot's boy

I heard them coming fast:

Dear Lord in Heaven! it was a joy,

The dead men could not blast.   540

I saw a third—I heard his voice:

It is the Hermit good!

He singeth loud his godly hymns

That he makes in the wood.

He'll shrieve my soul, he'll wash away

The Albatross's blood.

1holy rood] The cross of the Crucifixion.

1The moonlight ... shore] 1800: lines 481–502 deleted.

VII

This Hermit good lives in that wood

Which slopes down to the Sea.

How loudly his sweet voice he rears!

He loves to talk with Marineres 550

That come from a far Contrée.

He kneels at morn and noon and eve—

He hath a cushion plump:

It is the moss, that wholly hides

The rotted old Oak-stump.

The Skiff-boat ner'd: I heard them talk,

"Why, this is strange, I trow!

Where are those lights so many and fair

That signal made but now?"

"Strange, by my faith!" the Hermit said— 560

"And they answer'd not our cheer.

The planks look warp'd, and see those sails

How thin they are and sere!

I never saw aught like to them

Unless perchance it were

The skeletons of leaves that lag

My forest brook along:

When the Ivy-tod1 is heavy with snow,

And the Owlet whoops to the wolf below

That eats the she-wolf's young." 570

"Dear Lord! it has a fiendish look—"

(The Pilot made reply)

"I am a-fear'd."—"Push on, push on!"

Said the Hermit cheerily.

The Boat came closer to the Ship,

But I ne spake ne stirr'd!

The Boat came close beneath the Ship,

And strait a sound was heard!

Under the water it rumbled on,

Still louder and more dread: 580

It reach'd the Ship, it split the bay;

The Ship went down like lead.

Stunn'd by that loud and dreadful sound,

Which sky and ocean smote:

Like one that hath been seven days drown'd

My body lay afloat:

But, swift as dreams, myself I found

Within the Pilot's boat.

Upon the whirl, where sank the Ship,

The boat spun round and round: 590

And all was still, save that the hill

Was telling of the sound.

I mov'd my lips: the Pilot shriek'd

And fell down in a fit.

The Holy Hermit rais'd his eyes

And pray'd where he did sit.

I took the oars: the Pilot's boy,

Who now doth crazy go,

Laugh'd loud and long, and all the while

His eyes went to and fro,   600
"Ha! ha!" quoth he—"full plain I see,
The devil knows how to row."
And now all in mine own Countrée
I stood on the firm land!
The Hermit stepp'd forth from the boat,
And scarcely he could stand.
"O shrieve me, shrieve me, holy Man!"
The Hermit cross'd his brow—
"Say quick," quoth he, "I bid thee say

What manner man art thou?"   610
Forthwith this frame of mine was wrench'd
With a woeful agony,
Which forc'd me to begin my tale
And then it left me free.
Since then at an uncertain hour,
Now oftimes and now fewer,
That anguish comes and makes me tell
My ghastly aventure.1
I pass, like night, from land to land;

I have strange power of speech;   620
The moment that his face I see
I know the man that must hear me;
To him my tale I teach.

Eftsones] Again. 1800: "But soon"

Then ... blew] 1800: lines 531-36 deleted.

1Ivy-tod] An ivy bush; also, a place of concealment.

Now ... aventure] 1800: "That agony returns;/And till my ghastly tale is told/This heart within me burns."

What loud uproar bursts from that door! The Wedding-guests are there; But in the Garden-bower the Bride

And Bride-maids singing are:

And hark the little Vesper-bell

Which biddeth me to prayer.

O Wedding-guest! this soul hath been   630

Alone on a wide wide sea:

So lonely 'twas, that God himself

Scarce seemed there to be.

O sweeter than the Marriage-feast,

'Tis sweeter far to me

To walk together to the Kirk

With a goodly company.

To walk together to the Kirk

And all together pray,

While each to his great father bends,   640

Old men, and babes, and loving friends,

And Youths, and Maidens gay.

Farewell, farewell! but this I tell

To thee, thou wedding-guest!

He prayeth well who loveth well

Both man and bird and beast.

He prayeth best who loveth best,

All things both great and small:

For the dear God, who loveth us,

He made and loveth all.   650

The Marinere, whose eye is bright,

Whose beard with age is hoar,

Is gone; and now the wedding-guest

Turn'd from the bridegroom's door.

He went, like one that hath been stunn'd

And is of sense forlorn:

A sadder and a wiser man

He rose the morrow morn.

THE

FOSTER-MOTHER'S TALE,

A DRAMATIC FRAGMENT1

FOSTER-MOTHER

I never saw the man whom you describe.

MARIA

'Tis strange! he spake of you familiarly

As mine and Albert's common Foster-mother.

FOSTER-MOTHER

Now blessings on the man, whoe'er he be,

That joined your names with mine! O my sweet lady,

As often as I think of those dear times

When you two little ones would stand at eve

On each side of my chair, and make me learn

All you had learnt in the day; and how to talk

In gentle phrase, then bid me sing to you— 10 'Tis more like heaven to come than what has been.

MARIA

O my dear Mother! this strange man has left me

Troubled with wilder fancies, than the moon

Breeds in the love-sick maid who gazes at it,

Till lost in inward vision, with wet eye

She gazes idly! —But that entrance, Mother!

FOSTER-MOTHER

Can no one hear? It is a perilous tale!

By Coleridge; from the play Osorio, composed 1797 and revised as Remorse, which debuted at the Drury Lane Theatre in 1813. 1800: title changed to "The Foster-Mother's Tale. A Narration in Dramatic Blank Verse" and lines 1–16 deleted.

MARIA

No one.

FOSTER-MOTHER

My husband's father told it me,

Poor old Leoni!—Angels rest his soul!

He was a woodman, and could fell and saw   20

With lusty arm. You know that huge round beam

Which props the hanging wall of the old chapel?

Beneath that tree, while yet it was a tree

He found a baby wrapt in mosses, lined

With thistle-beards, and such small locks of wool

As hang on brambles. Well, he brought him home,

And reared him at the then Lord Velez' cost.

And so the babe grew up a pretty boy,

A pretty boy, but most unteachable—

And never learnt a prayer, nor told a bead,   30

But knew the names of birds, and mocked their notes,

And whistled, as he were a bird himself:1

And all the autumn 'twas his only play

To get the seeds of wild flowers, and to plant them

With earth and water, on the stumps of trees.

A Friar, who gathered simples2 in the wood,

A grey-haired man—he loved this little boy,

The boy loved him—and, when the Friar taught him,

He soon could write with the pen: and from that time,

Lived chiefly at the Convent or the Castle.   40

So he became a very learned youth.

But Oh! poor wretch!—he read, and read, and read, 'Till his brain turned—and ere his twentieth year, He had unlawful thoughts of many things:

And though he prayed, he never loved to pray With holy men, nor in a holy place—

But yet his speech, it was so soft and sweet, The late Lord Velez ne'er was wearied with him.

But ... himself] Wordsworth suggests a similar relationship between nature, bird-mimicry, and a young boy in "There was a boy." See p. 299. See also the excerpt from Joanna Baillie's De Monfort in Appendix G, pp. 526–27.

simples] Medicinal plants or herbs.

And once, as by the north side of the Chapel

They stood together, chained in deep discourse,   50

The earth heaved under them with such a groan,

That the wall tottered, and had well-nigh fallen

Right on their heads. My Lord was sorely frightened;

A fever seized him, and he made confession

Of all the heretical and lawless talk

Which brought this judgment: so the youth was seized

And cast into that hole. My husband's father

Sobbed like a child—it almost broke his heart:

And once as he was working in the cellar,

He heard a voice distinctly; 'twas the youth's,   60

Who sung a doleful song about green fields,

How sweet it were on lake or wild savannah,

To hunt for food, and be a naked man,

And wander up and down at liberty.1

He always doted on the youth, and now

His love grew desperate; and defying death,

He made that cunning entrance I described:

And the young man escaped.

MARIA

'Tis a sweet tale:

Such as would lull a listening child to sleep,

His rosy face besoiled with unwiped tears.—2

And what became of him?
FOSTER-MOTHER

He went on ship-board

With those bold voyagers, who made discovery

Of golden lands. Leoni's younger brother

Went likewise, and when he returned to Spain,

He told Leoni, that the poor mad youth,

Soon after they arrived in that new world,

In spite of his dissuasion, seized a boat,

And all alone, set sail by silent moonlight

How ... liberty] Most likely referring to the happy state of the "noble savage," popularized by Jean-Jacques Rousseau in his Discourse on the Origin of Inequality (1755).

Such ... tears] 1800: deleted.

Up a great river, great as any sea,

And ne'er was heard of more: but 'tis supposed, 80 He lived and died among the savage men.

LINES LEFT UPON A SEAT IN A YEW-TREE

WHICH STANDS NEAR THE LAKE OF ESTHWAITE,1

ON A DESOLATE PART OF THE SHORE,

YET COMMANDING A BEAUTIFUL PROSPECT2

—Nay, Traveller! rest. This lonely yew-tree stands Far from all human dwelling: what if here No sparkling rivulet spread the verdant herb;

What if these barren boughs the bee not loves;

Yet, if the wind breathe soft, the curling waves,

That break against the shore, shall lull thy mind

By one soft impulse saved from vacancy.

—————————————Who he was

That piled these stones, and with the mossy sod

First covered o'er, and taught this aged tree,   10

Now wild, to bend its arms in circling shade,

I well remember.—He was one who own'd

No common soul. In youth, by genius nurs'd,

And big with lofty views, he to the world

Went forth, pure in his heart,3 against the taint

Of dissolute tongues, 'gainst jealousy, and hate,

And scorn, against all enemies prepared,

All but neglect:4 and so, his spirit damped At once, with rash disdain he turned away,

Lake of Esthwaite] Located in the Lake District half a mile south of Hawkshead. See Appendix H, pp. 544–45.

By Wordsworth.

In youth ... heart] 1800: "In youth by science nursed/And led by nature into a wild scene/Of lofty hopes, he to the world went forth,/A favored being, knowing no desire/Which genius did not hallow,"

All but neglect] Here, the 1800 edition inserts: "The world, for so it

thought,/Owed him no service: he was like a plant/Fair to the sun, the darling of the winds,/But hung with fruit which no one, that passed by,/Regarded,"

And with the food of pride sustained his soul   20

In solitude.—Stranger! these gloomy boughs

Had charms for him; and here he loved to sit,

His only visitants a straggling sheep,

The stone-chat, or the glancing sand-piper;

And on these barren rocks, with juniper,

And heath, and thistle, thinly sprinkled o'er,

Fixing his downward eye, he many an hour

A morbid pleasure nourished, tracing here

An emblem of his own unfruitful life:

And lifting up his head, he then would gaze   30

On the more distant scene; how lovely 'tis

Thou seest, and he would gaze till it became

Far lovelier, and his heart could not sustain

The beauty still more beauteous. Nor, that time,1

Would he forget those beings, to whose minds,

Warm from the labours of benevolence,

The world, and man himself, appeared a scene

Of kindred loveliness: then he would sigh

With mournful joy, to think that others felt

What he must never feel: and so, lost man!   40

On visionary views would fancy feed,

Till his eye streamed with tears. In this deep vale

He died, this seat his only monument.

If thou be one whose heart the holy forms

Of young imagination have kept pure,

Stranger! henceforth be warned; and know, that pride,

Howe'er disguised in its own majesty,

Is littleness; that he, who feels contempt

For any living thing, hath faculties

Which he has never used; that thought with him 50

Is in its infancy. The man, whose eye

Is ever on himself, doth look on one,

The least of nature's works, one who might move

The wise man to that scorn which wisdom holds

Unlawful, ever. O, be wiser thou!

Instructed that true knowledge leads to love,

True dignity abides with him alone

Who, in the silent hour of inward thought,

Can still suspect, and still revere himself,

In lowliness of heart. 60

Nor, that time] Here, the 1800 edition inserts: "When Nature had subdued him to herself,"

THE NIGHTINGALE;

A CONVERSATIONAL POEM, WRITTEN IN APRIL,

1798[1]

No cloud, no relique of the sunken day

Distinguishes the West, no long thin slip

Of sullen Light, no obscure trembling hues.

Come, we will rest on this old mossy Bridge!

You see the glimmer of the stream beneath,

But hear no murmuring: it flows silently

O'er its soft bed of verdure. All is still,

A balmy night! and tho' the stars be dim,

Yet let us think upon the vernal showers

That gladden the green earth, and we shall find   10

A pleasure in the dimness of the stars.

And hark! the Nightingale begins its song, "Most musical, most melancholy"* Bird! A melancholy Bird? O idle thought! In nature there is nothing melancholy.

—But some night-wandering Man, whose heart was pierc'd With the remembrance of a grievous wrong, Or slow distemper or neglected love,

(And so, poor Wretch! fill'd all things with himself

"Most musical, most melancholy." This passage in Milton possesses an excellence far superior to that of mere description: it is spoken in the character of the melancholy Man, and has therefore a dramatic propri-ety. The Author makes this remark, to rescue himself from the charge of having alluded with levity to a line in Milton: a charge than which none could be more painful to him, except perhaps that of having ridiculed his Bible. [Coleridge's note. Coleridge refers to lines 61–64 of John Milton's Il Pensoroso (1645): "Sweet bird, that shunn'st the noise of folly,/Most musical, most melancholy!/ Thee, chauntress, oft the woods among/I woo, to hear thy even-song;"]

By Coleridge. The 1800 edition drops "A Conversational Poem" from the title.

And made all gentle sounds tell back the tale   20

Of his own sorrows) he and such as he

First nam'd these notes a melancholy strain;

And many a poet echoes the conceit,

Poet, who hath been building up the rhyme

When he had better far have stretch'd his limbs

Beside a brook in mossy forest-dell

By sun or moonlight, to the influxes

Of shapes and sounds and shifting elements

Surrendering his whole spirit, of his song

And of his fame forgetful! so his fame   30

Should share in nature's immortality,

A venerable thing! and so his song

Should make all nature lovelier, and itself

Be lov'd, like nature! —But 'twill not be so;

And youths and maidens most poetical

Who lose the deep'ning twilights of the spring

In ball-rooms and hot theatres, they still

Full of meek sympathy must heave their sighs

O'er Philomela's1 pity-pleading strains.

My Friend, and my Friend's Sister! we have learnt   40

A different lore: we may not thus profane

Nature's sweet voices always full of love

And joyance! 'Tis the merry Nightingale

That crowds, and hurries, and precipitates

With fast thick warble his delicious notes,

As he were fearful, that an April night

Would be too short for him to utter forth

His love-chant, and disburthen his full soul

Of all its music! And I know a grove

Of large extent, hard by a castle huge   50

Which the great lord inhabits not: and so

This grove is wild with tangling underwood,

Philomela's] Referring to a popular story in Greek mythology and in Ovid's Metamorphoses. Philomela and Procne were the daughters of King Pandion of Athens. Procne married King Tereus of Thrace, who raped Philomela and cut her out tongue. Though she could not speak, Philomela wove a tapestry to convey her betrayal to Procne. To revenge herself on Tereus, Procne killed and cooked their son Itys, but Tereus discovered the trick and pursued the sisters. Before he could catch them, all three were turned into birds: Tereus became a hoopoe, Procne a swallow, and Philomela a nightingale.

And the trim1 walks are broken up, and grass,

Thin grass and king-cups2 grow within the paths.

But never elsewhere in one place I knew

So many Nightingales: and far and near

In wood and thicket over the wide grove

They answer and provoke each other's songs—

With skirmish and capricious passagings,

And murmurs musical and swift jug jug   60

And one low piping sound more sweet than all—

Stirring the air with such an harmony,

That should you close your eyes, you might almost

Forget it was not day! On moonlight bushes,

Whose dewy leafits are but half disclos'd,

You may perchance behold them on the twigs,

Their bright, bright eyes, their eyes both bright and full,

Glistning, while many a glow-worm in the shade

Lights up her love-torch.3

A most gentle maid

Who dwelleth in her hospitable home   70

Hard by the Castle, and at latest eve,

(Even like a Lady vow'd and dedicate

To something more than nature in the grove)4

Glides thro' the pathways; she knows all their notes,

That gentle Maid! and oft, a moment's space,

What time the moon was lost behind a cloud,

Hath heard a pause of silence: till the Moon

Emerging, hath awaken'd earth and sky

With one sensation, and those wakeful Birds

Have all burst forth in choral minstrelsy,5   80

As if one quick and sudden Gale had swept

An hundred airy harps! And she hath watch'd

Many a Nightingale perch giddily

On blosmy twig still swinging from the breeze,

And to that motion tune his wanton song,

Like tipsy Joy that reels with tossing head.

trim] Neatly arrayed or dressed.

king-cups] In England, the name given to the common buttercup.

On moonlight ... love-torch] 1800: deleted.

Even ... grove] Echoing lines 23–32 of Coleridge's "Christabel." See Appendix B, p. 436.

minstrelsy] Harmony.

Farewell, O Warbler! till to-morrow eve,

And you, my friends! farewell, a short farewell!

We have been loitering long and pleasantly,

And now for our dear homes.—That strain again!   90

Full fain would it delay me!—My dear Babe,

Who, capable of no articulate sound,

Mars all things with his imitative lisp,

How he would place his hand beside his ear,

His little hand, the small forefinger up,

And bid us listen! And I deem it wise

To make him Nature's playmate. He knows well

The evening star: and once when he awoke

In most distressful mood (some inward pain

Had made up that strange thing, an infant's dream)   100

I hurried with him to our orchard plot,

And he beholds the moon, and hush'd at once

Suspends his sobs, and laughs most silently,

While his fair eyes that swam with undropt tears

Did glitter in the yellow moon-beam! Well—

It is a father's tale. But if that Heaven

Should give me life, his childhood shall grow up

Familiar with these songs, that with the night

He may associate Joy! Once more farewell,

Sweet Nightingale! once more, my friends! farewell.   110

THE
FEMALE VAGRANT1

By Derwent's side2 my Father's cottage stood, (The Woman thus her artless story told)

One field, a flock, and what the neighbouring flood

Supplied, to him were more than mines of gold.

Light was my sleep; my days in transport roll'd:

With thoughtless joy I stretch'd along the shore

My father's nets, or watched, when from the fold

High o'er the cliffs I led my fleecy store,

A dizzy depth below! his boat and twinkling oar.1

My father was a good and pious man,   10

An honest man by honest parents bred,

And I believe that, soon as I began

To lisp, he made me kneel beside my bed,

And in his hearing there my prayers I said:

And afterwards, by my good father taught,

I read, and loved the books in which I read;

For books in every neighbouring house I sought,

And nothing to my mind a sweeter pleasure brought.

Can I forget what charms did once adorn

My garden, stored with pease, and mint, and thyme,   20

And rose and lily for the sabbath morn?2

The sabbath bells, and their delightful chime;

The gambols and wild freaks3 at shearing time;

My hen's rich nest through long grass scarce espied;

The cowslip-gathering4 at May's dewy prime;

The swans, that, when I sought the water-side,

By Wordsworth; from Salisbury Plain, a long poem begun in 1793 and revised several times, until finally published as Guilt and Sorrow (1842).

By Derwent's side] Derwent Water lies immediately south of Keswick in the Lake District.

From far to meet me came, spreading their snowy pride.

The staff I yet remember which upbore The bending body of my active sire;

His seat beneath the honeyed sycamore   30

When the bees hummed, and chair by winter fire;

When market-morning came, the neat attire

With which, though bent on haste, myself I deck'd;

My watchful dog, whose starts of furious ire,

When stranger passed, so often I have check'd;

The suns of twenty summers danced along,—

Ah! little marked, how fast they rolled away:

Then rose a mansion proud our woods among,

And cottage after cottage owned its sway, 40 No joy to see a neighbouring house, or stray

Through pastures not his own, the master took; My Father dared his greedy wish gainsay;

He loved his old hereditary nook,1

And ill could I the thought of such sad parting brook.

But, when he had refused the proffered gold, To cruel injuries he became a prey,

Sore traversed2 in whate'er he bought and sold:

His troubles grew upon him day by day,

Till all his substance fell into decay. 50 His little range of water was denied;*

All but the bed where his old body lay,

All, all was seized, and weeping, side by side,

We sought a home where we uninjured might abide.3

The red-breast known for years, which at my casement peck'd.

High ... oar] 1800: "Saw on the distant lake his twinkling oar/Or watch'd his lazy boat still less'ning more and more."

And rose and lily for the sabbath morn] The rose cross originated as a Christian symbol in the first century and symbolized the redemptive power of Christ. In medieval iconography, the lily, in the form of a fleur-de-lis, often represented the trinity.

gambols and wild freaks] Dancing or capering; also games or capricious tricks.

cowslip-gathering] "Cowslip" is the common name of Primula veris, or marsh marigold. It is gathered in the spring, and its yellow blossoms are used to make wine.

Can I forget that miserable hour,

When from the last hill-top, my sire surveyed,

Peering above the trees, the steeple tower,

That on his marriage-day sweet music made?

Till then he hoped his bones might there be laid,

Close by my mother in their native bowers: 60 Bidding me trust in God, he stood and prayed,—

I could not pray:—through tears that fell in showers, Glimmer'd our dear-loved home, alas! no longer ours!

There was a youth whom I had loved so long, That when I loved him not I cannot say.

Several of the Lakes in the north of England are let out to different Fishermen, in parcels marked out by imaginary lines drawn from rock to rock. [Wordsworth's note]

'Mid the green mountains many and many a song We two had sung, like little1 birds in May.

When we began to tire of childish play

We seemed still more and more to prize each other:

We talked of marriage and our marriage day; 70 And I in truth did love him like a brother,

For never could I hope to meet with such another.

His father said, that to a distant town

He must repair, to ply the artist's trade.2

What tears of bitter grief till then unknown!

What tender vows our last sad kiss delayed!

To him we turned:—we had no other aid.

Like one revived, upon his neck I wept,

And her whom he had loved in joy, he said

old hereditary nook] See Wordsworth's 14 January 1801 letter to Charles James Fox, Appendix C, pp. 459–61.

traversed] Thwarted or opposed.

Then rose ... abide] Likely drawing on chapter nine of William Godwin's Caleb Williams (1794), which Wordsworth read while rewriting Salisbury Plain.

He well could love in grief: his faith he kept; 80 And in a quiet home once more my father slept.

Four years each day with daily bread was blest,

By constant toil and constant prayer supplied.

Three lovely infants lay upon my breast;

And often, viewing their sweet smiles, I sighed,

And knew not why. My happy father died

When sad distress reduced the children's meal:

Thrice happy! That from him the grave did hide

The empty loom, cold hearth, and silent wheel,

And tears that flowed for ills which patience could not heal.   90

'Twas a hard change, an evil time was come;3 We had no hope, and no relief could gain. But soon, with proud parade, the noisy drum Beat round, to sweep the streets of want and pain. My husband's arms now only served to strain Me and his children hungering in his view:

In such dismay my prayers and tears were vain:

To join those miserable men he flew;

And now to the sea-coast, with numbers more, we drew.

There foul neglect for months and months we bore,   100

Nor yet the crowded fleet its anchor stirred.

Green fields before us and our native shore,

By fever, from polluted air incurred,

Ravage was made, for which no knell was heard.

Fondly we wished, and wished away, nor knew,

'Mid that long sickness, and those hopes deferr'd,

That happier days we never more must view:

The parting signal1 streamed, at last the land withdrew,

But from delay the summer calms were past.

On as we drove, the equinoctial deep   110

Ran mountains-high before the howling blast.2

We gazed with terror on the gloomy sleep

Of them that perished in the whirlwind's sweep,

Untaught that soon such anguish must ensue,

Our hopes such harvest of affliction reap,

That we the mercy of the waves should rue.

We reached the western world, a poor, devoted crew.

Oh! dreadful price of being to resign

All that is dear in being! better far

In Want's most lonely cave till death to pine,   120

Unseen, unheard, unwatched by any star;

Or in the streets and walks where proud men are,

Better our dying bodies to obtrude,

Than dog-like, wading at the heels of war,

Protract a curst existence, with the brood

That lap (their very nourishment!) their brother's blood.

The pains and plagues that on our heads came down,

Disease and famine, agony and fear,

In wood or wilderness, in camp or town,

It would thy brain unsettle even to hear.   130

All perished—all, in one remorseless year,

Husband and children! one by one, by sword

And ravenous plague, all perished: every tear

Dried up, despairing, desolate, on board

A British ship I waked, as from a trance restored.

Peaceful as some immeasurable plain

By the first beams of dawning light impress'd,

In the calm sunshine slept the glittering main.

The very ocean has its hour of rest,

little] 1800: "gladsome"

Artist's] Craftsman's or artisan's.

an evil time was come] Food shortages and low wages plagued Britain in the late eighteenth century, particularly in the 1770s and in 1794–95.

parting signal] A flag flying from a ship indicating departure.

equinoctial deep ... howling blast] The autumnal equinox, when the day and night are of equal length all over the earth and tropical storms are common in the Atlantic.

That comes not to the human mourner's breast. 140

Remote from man, and storms of mortal care,

A heavenly silence did the waves invest;

I looked and looked along the silent air,

Until it seemed to bring a joy to my despair.

Ah! how unlike those late terrific sleeps!

And groans, that rage of racking famine spoke,

Where looks inhuman dwelt on festering heaps!

The breathing pestilence1 that rose like smoke!

The shriek that from the distant battle broke!

The mine's dire earthquake,2 and the pallid host 150 Driven by the bomb's incessant thunder-stroke

To loathsome vaults, where heart-sick anguish toss'd, Hope died, and fear itself in agony was lost!

Yet does that burst of woe congeal my frame,

When the dark streets appeared to heave and gape,

While like a sea the storming army came, And Fire from Hell reared his gigantic shape, And Murder, by the ghastly gleam, and Rape Seized their joint prey, the mother and the child!

But from these crazing thoughts my brain, escape! 160 —For weeks the balmy air breathed soft and mild, And on the gliding vessel Heaven and Ocean smiled.

Some mighty gulph of separation past,

I seemed transported to another world:—

A thought resigned with pain, when from the mast The impatient mariner the sail unfurl'd,

And whistling, called the wind that hardly curled

The silent sea. From the sweet thoughts of home,

And from all hope I was forever hurled.

For me—farthest from earthly port to roam 170 Was best, could I but shun the spot where man might come.

And oft, robb'd of my perfect mind, I thought

At last my feet a resting-place had found:

Here will I weep in peace, (so fancy wrought,)

Roaming the illimitable waters round;

Here watch, of every human friend disowned,

All day, my ready tomb the ocean-flood—

To break my dream the vessel reached its bound:

And homeless near a thousand homes I stood,

And near a thousand tables pined, and wanted food.   180

By grief enfeebled was I turned adrift,

Helpless as sailor cast on desart rock;

Nor morsel to my mouth that day did lift,

Nor dared my hand at any door to knock.

I lay, where with his drowsy mates, the cock

From the cross timber of an out-house hung;

How dismal tolled, that night, the city clock!

At morn my sick heart hunger scarcely stung,

Nor to the beggar's language could I frame my tongue.

So passed another day, and so the third: 190

Then did I try, in vain, the crowd's resort,

In deep despair by frightful wishes stirr'd,

Near the sea-side I reached a ruined fort:

There, pains which nature could no more support,

With blindness linked, did on my vitals fall;

Dizzy my brain, with interruption short

Of hideous sense; I sunk, nor step could crawl,

And thence was borne away to neighbouring hospital.

Recovery came with food: but still, my brain

Was weak, nor of the past had memory. 200 I heard my neighbours, in their beds, complain

Of many things which never troubled me; Of feet still bustling round with busy glee,

Of looks where common kindness had no part,

Of service done with careless cruelty,

Fretting the fever round the languid heart,

And groans, which, as they said, would make a dead man start.

These things just served to stir the torpid sense, Nor pain nor pity in my bosom raised.

Memory, though slow, returned with strength; and thence   210

Dismissed, again on open day I gazed,

At houses, men, and common light, amazed.

The lanes I sought, and as the sun retired,

Came, where beneath the trees a faggot blazed;

The wild brood saw me weep, my fate enquired,

And gave me food, and rest, more welcome, more desired.

My heart is touched to think that men like these,

The rude earth's tenants, were my first relief:

How kindly did they paint their vagrant ease!

And their long holiday that feared not grief, 220 For all belonged to all, and each was chief.

No plough their sinews strained; on grating road

No wain1 they drove, and yet, the yellow sheaf2

In every vale for their delight was stowed:

For them, in nature's meads,3 the milky udder flowed.

Semblance, with straw and panniered4 ass, they made

Of potters wandering on from door to door:

But life of happier sort to me pourtrayed, And other joys my fancy to allure;

The bag-pipe dinning on the midnight moor   230

In barn uplighted, and companions boon

Well met from far with revelry secure,

In depth of forest glade, when jocund June

Rolled fast along the sky his warm and genial moon.

But ill it suited me, in journey dark breathing pestilence] Eighteenth-century theories of contagion posited that breathing bad air could cause infection.

Mine's dire earthquake] Precursors to modern land mines were used as early as the Battle of Agincourt in 1415.

O'er moor and mountain, midnight theft to hatch;

To charm the surly house-dog's faithful bark,

Or hang on tiptoe at the lifted latch;

The gloomy lantern, and the dim blue match,

The black disguise,5 the warning whistle shrill,   240

And ear still busy on its nightly watch,

Were not for me, brought up in nothing ill;

Besides, on griefs so fresh my thoughts were brooding still.

What could I do, unaided and unblest?

Poor Father! gone was every friend of thine:

And kindred of dead husband are at best

Small help, and, after marriage such as mine,

With little kindness would to me incline.

Ill was I then for toil or service fit:

With tears whose course no effort could confine,   250

By high-way side forgetful would I sit

Whole hours, my idle arms in moping sorrow knit.

I lived upon the mercy of the fields,

And oft of cruelty the sky accused;

On hazard, or what general bounty yields,

Now coldly given, now utterly refused.

The fields I for my bed have often used:

But, what afflicts my peace with keenest ruth1

Is, that I have my inner self abused,

Foregone the home delight of constant truth,   260

And clear and open soul, so prized in fearless youth.

Three years a wanderer, often have I view'd,

In tears, the sun towards that country tend

Where my poor heart lost all its fortitude:

And now across this moor my steps I bend—

Oh! tell me whither——for no earthly friend

Have I.——She ceased, and weeping turned away,

As if because her tale was at an end

She wept;—because she had no more to say

Of that perpetual weight which on her spirit lay.   270

wain] An open vehicle drawn by horses or oxen for transporting agricul-tural produce.

sheaf] A bundle of wheat tied together after reaping.

meads] Meadows.

panniered ass] A donkey with a pair of baskets slung across its back.

The black disguise] The English statute 9 George I (1723), known com-monly as "the Black Act," made it a capital felony to hunt or steal deer or appear in a public park with the face blackened. It was repealed in 1827.

GOODY BLAKE,
AND
HARRY GILL,
A TRUE STORY2

Oh! what's the matter? what's the matter? What is't that ails young Harry Gill? That evermore his teeth they chatter,

Chatter, chatter, chatter still.

Of waistcoats Harry has no lack,

Good duffle grey, and flannel fine;

He has a blanket on his back,

And coats enough to smother nine.

In March, December, and in July,

'Tis all the same with Harry Gill; 10 The neighbours tell, and tell you truly, His teeth they chatter, chatter still.

At night, at morning, and at noon,

'Tis all the same with Harry Gill;

Beneath the sun, beneath the moon,

His teeth they chatter, chatter still.

Young Harry was a lusty drover,1

And who so stout of limb as he?

His cheeks were red as ruddy clover,

His voice was like the voice of three. 20 Auld2 Goody Blake was old and poor,

Ill fed she was, and thinly clad;

And any man who pass'd her door,

Might see how poor a hut she had.

All day she spun in her poor dwelling,

And then her three hours' work at night!

Alas! 'twas hardly worth the telling,

It would not pay for candle-light. —This woman dwelt in Dorsetshire,3

Her hut was on a cold hill-side, 30 And in that country4 coals are dear,

For they come far by wind and tide.

By the same fire to boil their pottage,5

Two poor old dames, as I have known,

Will often live in one small cottage,

But she, poor woman, dwelt alone.

'Twas well enough when summer came,

The long, warm, lightsome summer-day,

Then at her door the canty1 dame

Would sit, as any linnet2 gay.   40

But when the ice our streams did fetter,

Oh! then how her old bones would shake!

You would have said, if you had met her,

'Twas a hard time for Goody Blake.

Her evenings then were dull and dead;

Sad case it was, as you may think,

For very cold to go to bed,

And then for cold not sleep a wink.

Oh joy for her! when e'er in winter

The winds at night had made a rout,   50

And scatter'd many a lusty splinter,

And many a rotten bough about.

Yet never had she, well or sick,

As every man who knew her says,

A pile before-hand, wood or stick,

Enough to warm her for three days.

Now, when the frost was past enduring,

And made her poor old bones to ache,

Could any thing be more alluring,

Than an old hedge3 to Goody Blake?   60

And now and then, it must be said,

When her old bones were cold and chill,

She left her fire, or left her bed,

To seek the hedge of Harry Gill.

Now Harry he had long suspected

This trespass of old Goody Blake,

And vow'd that she should be detected,

And he on her would vengeance take.

And oft from his warm fire he'd go,

And to the fields his road would take,   70

And there, at night, in frost and snow,

He watch'd to seize old Goody Blake.

And once, behind a rick1 of barley,

Thus looking out did Harry stand;

The moon was full and shining clearly,

And crisp with frost the stubble-land.

—He hears a noise—he's all awake—

Again?—on tip-toe down the hill

He softly creeps—'Tis Goody Blake,

She's at the hedge of Harry Gill. 80

Right glad was he when he beheld her:

Stick after stick did Goody pull,

He stood behind a bush of elder,

Till she had filled her apron full.

When with her load she turned about,

The bye-road2 back again to take,

He started forward with a shout,

And sprang upon poor Goody Blake.

And fiercely by the arm he took her,

And by the arm he held her fast, 90

And fiercely by the arm he shook her,

And cried, "I've caught you then at last!"

Then Goody, who had nothing said,

Her bundle from her lap let fall;

And kneeling on the sticks, she pray'd

To God that is the judge of all.

She pray'd, her wither'd hand uprearing,

While Harry held her by the arm—

"God! who art never out of hearing,

O may he never more be warm!" 100

The cold, cold moon above her head,

Thus on her knees did Goody pray,

Young Harry heard what she had said,

And icy-cold he turned away.

He went complaining all the morrow

That he was cold and very chill:

His face was gloom, his heart was sorrow,

Alas! that day for Harry Gill!

That day he wore a riding-coat,

But not a whit the warmer he: 110

Another was on Thursday brought,

And ere the Sabbath he had three.

'Twas all in vain, a useless matter,

And blankets were about him pinn'd;

Yet still his jaws and teeth they clatter,

Like a loose casement in the wind.

And Harry's flesh it fell away;

And all who see him say 'tis plain,

That, live as long as live he may,

He never will be warm again. 120

No word to any man he utters,

A-bed or up, to young or old;

But ever to himself he mutters,

"Poor Harry Gill is very cold."

A-bed or up, by night or day;

His teeth they chatter, chatter still.

Now think, ye farmers all, I pray,

Of Goody Blake and Harry Gill.

ruth] Sorrow.

By Wordsworth. The story on which the poem is based first appeared in Erasmus
Darwin's Zoönomia; or,The Laws of Organic Life (1794–96). See Appendix F, p. 500.

drover] One who drives cattle or sheep to distant markets.

Auld] "Auld" is an archaic form of "Old"; it functions in this line both as adjective and as rustic title, mirroring "Young Harry" in line 17.

Dorsetshire] Erasmus Darwin's Zoönomia places the incident in Warwick-shire, and makes no mention of the price of fuel.

country] "County," in this context.

pottage] Thick soup.

canty] Cheerful, talkative.

linnet] A songbird common in Britain.

hedge] A row of bushes or low trees (usually hawthorn or privet) planted closely and pruned to form a natural fence between fields or between field and road.

rick] A regularly constructed stack.

bye-road] An unfrequented road.

LINES WRITTEN AT A SMALL DISTANCE FROM MY HOUSE, AND SENT BY MY LITTLE BOY TO THE PERSON TO WHOM THEY ARE ADDRESSED1

It is the first mild day of March:

Each minute sweeter than before,

The red-breast sings from the tall larch2

That stands beside our door.

There is a blessing in the air,

Which seems a sense of joy to yield

To the bare trees, and mountains bare,

And grass in the green field.

My Sister! ('tis a wish of mine)

Now that our morning meal is done,   10

Make haste, your morning task resign;

Come forth and feel the sun.

Edward will come with you, and pray,

Put on with speed your woodland dress,

And bring no book, for this one day

We'll give to idleness.

No joyless forms shall regulate

Our living Calendar:

We from to-day, my friend, will date

The opening of the year.   20

Love, now an universal birth,

From heart to heart is stealing,

From earth to man, from man to earth,

—It is the hour of feeling.

One moment now may give us more

Than fifty years of reason;

Our minds shall drink at every pore

The spirit of the season.

Some silent laws our hearts may make,

Which they shall long obey; 30

We for the year to come may take

Our temper from to-day.

And from the blessed power that rolls

About, below, above;

We'll frame the measure of our souls,

They shall be tuned to love.

Then come, my sister! come, I pray,

With speed put on your woodland dress,

And bring no book; for this one day

We'll give to idleness. 40

By Wordsworth.

larch] Coniferous tree native to the Alps but cultivated in Britain. Unlike other firs and pines, its needles turn golden in the late fall and drop off.

SIMON LEE, THE OLD HUNTSMAN,

WITH AN INCIDENT IN WHICH HE WAS CONCERNED1

In the sweet shire of Cardigan,2

Not far from pleasant Ivor-hall,

An old man dwells, a little man,

I've heard he once was tall.

Of years he has upon his back,

No doubt, a burthen weighty;

He says he is three score and ten,

But others say he's eighty.

A long blue livery-coat has he,

That's fair behind, and fair before;   10

Yet, meet him where you will, you see

At once that he is poor.

Full five and twenty years he lived

A running huntsman merry;

And, though he has but one eye left,

His cheek is like a cherry.

No man like him the horn could sound, And no man was so full of glee;

To say the least, four counties round

Had heard of Simon Lee; 20 His master's dead, and no one now Dwells in the hall of Ivor;

Men, dogs, and horses, all are dead;

He is the sole survivor.

His hunting feats have him bereft

Of his right eye, as you may see:

And then, what limbs those feats have left To poor old Simon Lee!

He has no son, he has no child,

His wife, an aged woman, 30 Lives with him, near the waterfall,

Upon the village common.

By Wordsworth.

Cardigan] A county in western Wales. See Appendix H, p. 542.

nd he is lean and he is sick,

His little1 body's half awry,

His ancles they are swoln and thick;

His legs are thin and dry.

When he was young he little knew

Of husbandry or tillage;

And now he's forced to work, though weak,

—The weakest in the village.   40

He all the country could outrun,

Could leave both man and horse behind;

And often, ere the race was done,

He reeled and was stone-blind.

And still there's something in the world

At which his heart rejoices;

For when the chiming hounds are out,

He dearly loves their voices!

Old Ruth works out of doors with him,

And does what Simon cannot do;   50

For she, not over stout of limb,

Is stouter of the two.

And though you with your utmost skill

From labour could not wean them,

Alas! 'tis very little, all

Which they can do between them.

Beside their moss-grown hut of clay,

Not twenty paces from the door,

A scrap of land they have, but they

Are poorest of the poor. 60

This scrap of land he from the heath

Enclosed when he was stronger;

But what avails the land to them,

Which they can till no longer?

Few months of life has he in store,

As he to you will tell,

For still, the more he works, the more

His poor old ancles swell.2

little] 1800: "dwindled"

ancles swell] A symptom of edema, commonly called "dropsy" in the eighteenth
century.

My gentle reader, I perceive

How patiently you've waited, 70

And I'm afraid that you expect

Some tale will be related.

O reader! had you in your mind

Such stores as silent thought can bring,

O gentle reader! you would find

A tale in every thing.

What more I have to say is short,

I hope you'll kindly take it;

It is no tale; but should you think,

Perhaps a tale you'll make it.   80

One summer-day I chanced to see

This old man doing all he could

About the root of an old tree,

A stump of rotten wood.

The mattock1 totter'd in his hand;

So vain was his endeavour

That at the root of the old tree

He might have worked for ever.

"You're overtasked, good Simon Lee,

Give me your tool" to him I said;   90

And at the word right gladly he

Received my proffer'd aid.

I struck, and with a single blow

The tangled root I sever'd,

At which the poor old man so long

And vainly had endeavour'd.

The tears into his eyes were brought,

And thanks and praises seemed to run

So fast out of his heart, I thought

They never would have done.   100

—I've heard of hearts unkind, kind deeds

With coldness still returning.

Alas! the gratitude of men

Has oftner left me mourning.

mattock] A tool similar to a pick with a chisel edge on one head used for breaking ground or removing tree stumps.

.ANECDOTE FOR FATHERS,
SHEWING HOW THE ART OF LYING MAY BE TAUGHT1

I have a boy of five years old,

His face is fair and fresh to see;

His limbs are cast in beauty's mould,

And dearly he loves me.

One morn we stroll'd on our dry walk,

Our quiet house all full in view,

And held such intermitted talk

As we are wont to do.

My thoughts on former pleasures ran;

I thought of Kilve's2 delightful shore,   10

My pleasant home, when spring began,

A long, long year before.

A day it was when I could bear

To think, and think, and think again;

With so much happiness to spare,

I could not feel a pain.

My boy was by my side, so slim

And graceful in his rustic dress!

And oftentimes I talked to him,

In very idleness.   20

The young lambs ran a pretty race;

The morning sun shone bright and warm; "Kilve," said I, "was a pleasant place, And so is Liswyn farm."3By Wordsworth.

Kilve] An English village on the Bristol Channel in the county of Som-erset. See Appendix H, p. 542.

Liswyn farm] Also "Llys Wen" farm. In a later note to this poem, Wordsworth explained that "The name of Liswyn farm was taken from a beautiful spot on the Wye [River]." In 1797, Coleridge, Wordsworth, and Dorothy Wordsworth visited the political radical and poet John Thelwall at Llys-Wen Farm in Wales. In 1811 this same farm became the home of Percy Shelley, who chose it largely because of its ties to Thelwall. See Appendix H, p. 542.

"My little boy, which like you more," I said and took him by the arm— "Our home by Kilve's delightful shore, Or here at Liswyn farm?"

"And tell me, had you rather be,"

I said and held him by the arm,   30

"At Kilve's smooth shore by the green sea,

Or here at Liswyn farm?"

In careless mood he looked at me,

While still I held him by the arm,

And said, "At Kilve I'd rather be

Than here at Liswyn farm."

"Now, little Edward, say why so;

My little Edward, tell me why;"

"I cannot tell, I do not know."

"Why this is strange," said I.   40

"For, here are woods and green-hills warm;

There surely must some reason be

Why you would change sweet Liswyn farm

For Kilve by the green sea."

At this, my boy, so fair and slim,

Hung down his head, nor made reply;

And five times did I say to him,

"Why? Edward, tell me why?"

His head he raised—there was in sight,

It caught his eye, he saw it plain—   50

Upon the house-top, glittering bright,

A broad and gilded vane.

Then did the boy his tongue unlock,

And thus to me he made reply;

"At Kilve there was no weather-cock,

And that's the reason why."

Oh dearest, dearest boy! my heart

For better lore would seldom yearn,

Could I but teach the hundredth part

Of what from thee I learn.   60

WE ARE SEVEN1

A simple child, dear brother Jim,
That lightly draws its breath,
And feels its life in every limb,
What should it know of death?
I met a little cottage girl,
She was eight years old, she said;
Her hair was thick with many a curl
That cluster'd round her head.
She had a rustic, woodland air,
And she was wildly clad;   10

Her eyes were fair, and very fair,
—Her beauty made me glad.
"Sisters and brothers, little maid,
How many may you be?"
"How many? seven in all," she said,
And wondering looked at me.
"And where are they, I pray you tell?"
She answered, "Seven are we,
And two of us at Conway2 dwell,
And two are gone to sea.   20

Two of us in the church-yard lie,
My sister and my brother,
And in the church-yard cottage, I
Dwell near them with my mother."

"You say that two at Conway dwell,

And two are gone to sea,

Yet you are seven; I pray you tell

Sweet Maid, how this may be?"

By Wordsworth.

Conway] A town on the Conway River estuary on the Northern coast of Wales. See
Appendix H, p. 542.

Then did the little Maid reply,

"Seven boys and girls are we;   30

Two of us in the church-yard lie,

Beneath the church-yard tree."

"You run about, my little maid,

Your limbs they are alive;

If two are in the church-yard laid,

Then ye are only five."

"Their graves are green, they may be seen,"

The little Maid replied,

"Twelve steps or more from my mother's door,

And they are side by side.   40

My stockings there I often knit,

My 'kerchief there I hem;

And there upon the ground I sit—

I sit and sing to them.

And often after sunset, Sir,

When it is light and fair,

I take my little porringer,

And eat my supper there.

The first that died was little Jane;

In bed she moaning lay, 50

Till God released her of her pain,

And then she went away.

So in the church-yard she was laid,

And all the summer dry,

Together round her grave we played,

My brother John and I.

And when the ground was white with snow,

And I could run and slide,

My brother John was forced to go,

And he lies by her side." 60

"How many are you then," said I,

"If they two are in Heaven?"

The little Maiden did reply,

"O Master! we are seven."

"But they are dead; those two are dead!

Their spirits are in heaven!"

'Twas throwing words away; for still

The little Maid would have her will,

And said, "Nay, we are seven!"

LINES WRITTEN IN EARLY SPRING1

I heard a thousand blended notes,

While in a grove I sate reclined,

In that sweet mood when pleasant thoughts

Bring sad thoughts to the mind.

To her fair works did nature link

The human soul that through me ran;

And much it griev'd my heart to think

What man has made of man.

Through primrose-tufts, in that sweet bower,

The periwinkle trail'd its wreathes;   10

And 'tis my faith that every flower

Enjoys the air it breathes.

The birds around me hopp'd and play'd:

Their thoughts I cannot measure,

But the least motion which they made,

It seem'd a thrill of pleasure.

The budding twigs spread out their fan,

To catch the breezy air;

And I must think, do all I can,

That there was pleasure there.   20

If I these thoughts may not prevent,

If such be of my creed the plan,

Have I not reason to lament

What man has made of man?

-By Wordsworth.

THE
THORN1

I

There is a thorn; it looks so old,

In truth you'd find it hard to say,

How it could ever have been young,

It looks so old and grey.

Not higher than a two-years' child,

It stands erect this aged thorn;

No leaves it has, no thorny points;

It is a mass of knotted joints,

A wretched thing forlorn.

It stands erect, and like a stone 10 With lichens it is overgrown.

II

Like rock or stone, it is o'ergrown

With lichens to the very top,

And hung with heavy tufts of moss,

A melancholy crop:

Up from the earth these mosses creep,

And this poor thorn they clasp it round

So close, you'd say that they were bent

With plain and manifest intent,

To drag it to the ground;   20

And all had joined in one endeavour

To bury this poor thorn for ever.

III

High on a mountain's highest ridge,

Where oft the stormy winter gale

Cuts like a scythe, while through the clouds

It sweeps from vale to vale;

Not five yards from the mountain-path,

This thorn you on your left espy;

And to the left, three yards beyond,

You see a little muddy pond   30

Of water, never dry;

I've measured it from side to side:

'Tis three feet long, and two feet wide.

IV

And close beside this aged thorn,

There is a fresh and lovely sight,

A beauteous heap, a hill of moss,

Just half a foot in height.

All lovely colours there you see,

All colours that were ever seen,

And mossy network too is there,   40

As if by hand of lady fair

The work had woven been,

And cups,1 the darlings of the eye,

So deep is their vermilion dye.

V

Ah me! what lovely tints are there!

Of olive-green and scarlet bright,

In spikes, in branches, and in stars,

Green, red, and pearly white.

This heap of earth o'ergrown with moss,

Which close beside the thorn you see,   50

So fresh in all its beauteous dyes,

Is like an infant's grave in size,

As like as like can be:

But never, never any where,

An infant's grave was half so fair.

VI

Now would you see this aged thorn,

This pond and beauteous hill of moss,

You must take care and chuse your time

The mountain when to cross.

For oft there sits, between the heap   60

That's like an infant's grave in size,

And that same pond of which I spoke,

A woman in a scarlet cloak,

And to herself she cries,

"Oh misery! oh misery!

Oh woe is me! oh misery!"

1By Wordsworth.

1cups] Blossoms.

VII

At all times of the day and night

This wretched woman thither goes,

And she is known to every star,

And every wind that blows;   70

And there beside the thorn she sits

When the blue day-light's in the skies,

And when the whirlwind's on the hill,

Or frosty air is keen and still,

And to herself she cries,

"Oh misery! oh misery!

Oh woe is me! oh misery!"

VIII

"Now wherefore thus, by day and night, In rain, in tempest, and in snow,

Thus to the dreary mountain-top 80 Does this poor woman go?

And why sits she beside the thorn

When the blue day-light's in the sky,

Or when the whirlwind's on the hill,

Or frosty air is keen and still,

And wherefore does she cry?—

Oh wherefore? wherefore? tell me why Does she repeat that doleful cry?"

IX

I cannot tell; I wish I could;

For the true reason no one knows,   90

But if you'd gladly view the spot,

The spot to which she goes;

The heap that's like an infant's grave, The pond—and thorn, so old and grey,

Pass by her door—'tis seldom shut—

And if you see her in her hut,

Then to the spot away!—

I never heard of such as dare

Approach the spot when she is there.

X

"But wherefore to the mountain-top   100

Can this unhappy woman go,

Whatever star is in the skies,

Whatever wind may blow?"

Nay rack your brain—'tis all in vain,

I'll tell you every thing I know;

But to the thorn, and to the pond

Which is a little step beyond,

I wish that you would go:

Perhaps when you are at the place

You something of her tale may trace.   110

XI

I'll give you the best help I can:

Before you up the mountain go,

Up to the dreary mountain-top,

I'll tell you all I know.

'Tis now some two and twenty years,

Since she (her name is Martha Ray1)

Gave with a maiden's true good will

Her company to Stephen Hill;

And she was blithe and gay,

And she was happy, happy still   120

Whene'er she thought of Stephen Hill.

XII

And they had fix'd the wedding-day,

The morning that must wed them both;

But Stephen to another maid

Had sworn another oath;

And with this other maid to church

Unthinking Stephen went—

Poor Martha! on that woful day

A cruel, cruel fire, they say,

Into her bones was sent: 130

It dried her body like a cinder,

And almost turn'd her brain to tinder.

XIII

They say, full six months after this,

While yet the summer-leaves were green,

She to the mountain-top would go,

And there was often seen.

'Tis said, a child was in her womb,

As now to any eye was plain;

She was with child, and she was mad,

Yet often she was sober sad 140

From her exceeding pain.

Oh me! ten thousand times I'd rather

That he had died, that cruel father!

XIV

Sad case for such a brain to hold

Communion with a stirring child!

Sad case, as you may think, for one

Who had a brain so wild!

Last Christmas when we talked of this,

Old Farmer Simpson did maintain,

That in her womb the infant wrought   150

About its mother's heart, and brought

Her senses back again:

And when at last her time drew near,

Her looks were calm, her senses clear.

XVI

And all that winter, when at night

The wind blew from the mountain-peak, 'Twas worth your while, though in the dark,
The church-yard path to seek:

For many a time and oft were heard   170

Cries coming from the mountain-head,

Some plainly living voices were,

And others, I've heard many swear,

Were voices of the dead:

I cannot think, whate'er they say,

They had to do with Martha Ray.

XVII

But that she goes to this old thorn,

The thorn which I've described to you,

And there sits in a scarlet cloak,

I will be sworn is true. 180 For one day with my telescope,

To view the ocean wide and bright,

When to this country first I came,

Ere I had heard of Martha's name,

I climbed the mountain's height:

A storm came on, and I could see

No object higher than my knee.

XVIII

'Twas mist and rain, and storm and rain,

No screen, no fence could I discover,

And then the wind! in faith, it was   190

A wind full ten times over.

I looked around, I thought I saw

A jutting crag, and off I ran,

Head-foremost, through the driving rain,

The shelter of the crag to gain,

And, as I am a man,

Instead of jutting crag, I found

A woman seated on the ground.

XIX

I did not speak—I saw her face,

Her face it was enough for me;   200

I turned about and heard her cry,

"O misery! O misery!"

And there she sits, until the moon

Through half the clear blue sky will go,

And when the little breezes make

The waters of the pond to shake,

As all the country know,

She shudders and you hear her cry,

"Oh misery! oh misery!"

XX

"But what's the thorn? and what's the pond?   210

And what's the hill of moss to her?

And what's the creeping breeze that comes

The little pond to stir?"

I cannot tell; but some will say

She hanged her baby on the tree,

Some say she drowned it in the pond,

Which is a little step beyond,

But all and each agree,

The little babe was buried there,

Beneath that hill of moss so fair.   220

Martha Ray] As with Liswyn Farm in "Anecdote for Fathers," Martha Ray of "The
Thorn" has a real-life counterpart in the mistress of John Montagu, Forth Earl
of Sandwich; Martha Ray was murdered 7 April 1779 by a rejected suitor, James
Hackman. Wordsworth's friend Basil Montagu (1770–1851) was the illegitimate son

of the Earl and Martha Ray; Wordsworth's ward Basil Montagu Jr. was their grandson.

XXI

I've heard the scarlet moss is red

With drops of that poor infant's blood;

But kill a new-born infant thus!

I do not think she could.

Some say, if to the pond you go,

And fix on it a steady view,

The shadow of a babe you trace,

A baby and a baby's face,

And that it looks at you;

Whene'er you look on it, 'tis plain 230 The baby looks at you again.

XXII

And some had sworn an oath that she

Should be to public justice brought;

And for the little infant's bones

With spades they would have sought.

But then the beauteous hill of moss

Before their eyes began to stir;

And for full fifty yards around,

The grass it shook upon the ground;

But all do still aver   240

The little babe is buried there,

Beneath that hill of moss so fair.

XXIII

I cannot tell how this may be,

But plain it is, the thorn is bound

With heavy tufts of moss, that strive

To drag it to the ground.

And this I know, full many a time,

When she was on the mountain high,

By day, and in the silent night,

When all the stars shone clear and bright,   250

That I have heard her cry,

"Oh misery! oh misery!

Oh woe is me! oh misery!"

THE LAST OF THE FLOCK1

In distant countries I have been,
And yet I have not often seen
A healthy man, a man full grown,
Weep in the public roads alone.
But such a one, on English ground,
And in the broad high-way, I met;
Along the broad high-way he came,
His cheeks with tears were wet.
Sturdy he seemed, though he was sad;
And in his arms a lamb he had.   10

He saw me, and he turned aside,
As if he wished himself to hide:
Then with his coat he made essay
To wipe those briny tears away.
I follow'd him, and said, "My friend
What ails you? wherefore weep you so?"
—"Shame on me, Sir! this lusty lamb,
He makes my tears to flow.
To-day I fetched him from the rock;
He is the last of all my flock.   20

When I was young, a single man,
And after youthful follies ran,
Though little given to care and thought,
Yet, so it was, a ewe I bought;
And other sheep from her I raised,
As healthy sheep as you might see,

And then I married, and was rich

As I could wish to be;

Of sheep I number'd a full score,

And every year encreas'd my store.   30

Year after year my stock it grew,

And from this one, this single ewe,

Full fifty comely sheep I raised,

1By Wordsworth.

As sweet a flock as ever grazed!

Upon the mountain did they feed;

They throve, and we at home did thrive.

—This lusty lamb of all my store

Is all that is alive:

And now I care not if we die,

And perish all of poverty.   40

Ten children, Sir! had I to feed,

Hard labour in a time of need!

My pride was tamed, and in our grief,

I of the parish ask'd relief.

They said I was a wealthy man;

My sheep upon the mountain fed,

And it was fit that thence I took

Whereof to buy us bread:

'Do this; how can we give to you,'

They cried, 'what to the poor is due?'   50

I sold a sheep as they had said,

And bought my little children bread,

And they were healthy with their food;

For me it never did me good.

A woeful time it was for me,

To see the end of all my gains,

The pretty flock which I had reared

With all my care and pains,

To see it melt like snow away!

For me it was woeful day. 60

Another still! and still another!

A little lamb, and then its mother!

It was a vein that never stopp'd,

Like blood-drops from my heart they dropp'd.

Till thirty were not left alive

They dwindled, dwindled, one by one,

And I may say that many a time

I wished they all were gone:

They dwindled one by one away;

For me it was a woeful day. 70

To wicked deeds I was inclined, And wicked fancies cross'd my mind,

And every man I chanc'd to see,

I thought he knew some ill of me.

No peace, no comfort could I find,

No ease, within doors or without,

And crazily, and wearily,

I went my work about.

Oft-times I thought to run away;

For me it was a woeful day. 80

Sir! 'twas a precious flock to me,

As dear as my own children be;

For daily with my growing store

I loved my children more and more.

Alas! it was an evil time;

God cursed me in my sore distress,

I prayed, yet every day I thought

I loved my children less;

And every week, and every day,

My flock, it seemed to melt away. 90

They dwindled, Sir, sad sight to see!

From ten to five, from five to three,

A lamb, a weather,1 and a ewe;

And then at last, from three to two;

And of my fifty, yesterday

I had but only one,

And here it lies upon my arm,

Alas! and I have none;

To-day I fetched it from the rock;

It is the last of all my flock." 100

THE DUNGEON2

And this place our forefathers made for man!

This is the process of our love and wisdom,

To each poor brother who offends against us—

Most innocent, perhaps—and what if guilty?

Is this the only cure? Merciful God!

Each pore and natural outlet shrivell'd up

By ignorance and parching poverty,

His energies roll back upon his heart,

And stagnate and corrupt; till changed to poison,

They break out on him, like a loathsome plague-spot;   10

Then we call in our pamper'd mountebanks1—

And this is their best cure! uncomforted

And friendless solitude, groaning and tears,

And savage faces, at the clanking hour,

Seen through the steams and vapour of his dungeon,

By the lamp's dismal twilight! So he lies

Circled with evil, till his very soul

Unmoulds its essence, hopelessly deformed

By sights of ever more deformity!

With other ministrations thou, O nature!   20

Healest thy wandering and distempered child:

Thou pourest on him thy soft influences,

Thy sunny hues, fair forms, and breathing sweets,

Thy melodies of woods, and winds, and waters,

Till he relent, and can no more endure

To be a jarring and a dissonant thing,

Amid this general dance and minstrelsy;2

But, bursting into tears, wins back his way,

His angry spirit healed and harmonized

By the benignant touch of love and beauty.   30

weather] Or "wether," a castrated male sheep.

By Coleridge. Extracted from the unpublished play Osorio, composed in 1797.

THE
MAD MOTHER3

Her eyes are wild, her head is bare,

The sun has burnt her coal-black hair,

Her eye-brows have a rusty stain,
And she came far from over the main.4

She has a baby on her arm,
Or else she were alone;
And underneath the hay-stack warm,
And on the green-wood stone,
She talked and sung the woods among;

And it was in the English tongue.   10
"Sweet babe! They say that I am mad,
But nay, my heart is far too glad;
And I am happy when I sing
Full many a sad and doleful thing:
Then, lovely baby, do not fear!
I pray thee have no fear of me,
But, safe as in a cradle, here
My lovely baby! thou shalt be,
To thee I know too much I owe;

I cannot work thee any woe.   20

A fire was once within my brain;

And in my head a dull, dull pain;

And fiendish faces one, two, three,

Hung at my breasts, and pulled at me.

But then there came a sight of joy;

It came at once to do me good;

I waked, and saw my little boy,

My little boy of flesh and blood;

Oh joy for me that sight to see!

For he was here, and only he.   30

Suck, little babe, oh suck again!

It cools my blood; it cools my brain;1

Thy lips I feel them, baby! they

Draw from my heart the pain away.

Oh! press me with thy little hand;

It loosens something at my chest;

About that tight and deadly band

I feel thy little fingers press'd.

The breeze I see is in the tree;

It comes to cool my babe and me.   40

mountebanks] Quack doctors.

minstrelsy] Harmony.

By Wordsworth.

main] Short for "main sea," meaning "open sea."

It cools my blood; it cools my brain] Ancient Greek physicians posited the brain as a cooling plant for the blood; the notion persisted through the seventeenth century but lost credit with eighteenth-century physicians.

Oh! love me, love me, little boy!

Thou art thy mother's only joy;

And do not dread the waves below,

When o'er the sea-rock's edge we go;

The high crag cannot work me harm,

Nor leaping torrents when they howl;

The babe I carry on my arm,

He saves for me my precious soul;

Then happy lie, for blest am I;

Without me my sweet babe would die.   50

Then do not fear, my boy! for thee

Bold as a lion I will be;

And I will always be thy guide,

Through hollow snows and rivers wide.

I'll build an Indian bower; I know

The leaves that make the softest bed:

And if from me thou wilt not go,

But still be true 'till I am dead,

My pretty thing! then thou shalt sing,

As merry as the birds in spring.   60

Thy father cares not for my breast,

'Tis thine, sweet baby, there to rest:

'Tis all thine own! and if its hue

Be changed, that was so fair to view,1

'Tis fair enough for thee, my dove!

My beauty, little child, is flown;

But thou wilt live with me in love,

And what if my poor cheek be brown?

'Tis well for me, thou canst not see

How pale and wan it else would be. 70

Dread not their taunts, my little life!

I am thy father's wedded wife;

And underneath the spreading tree

We two will live in honesty.

If his sweet boy he could forsake,

With me he never would have stay'd:

and ... view] Recalling lines 244–47 of Coleridge's "Christabel." See Appendix B, p. 441.

From him no harm my babe can take,

But he, poor man! is wretched made,

And every day we two will pray

For him that's gone and far away. 80

I'll teach my boy the sweetest things;

I'll teach him how the owlet sings.

My little babe! thy lips are still,

And thou hast almost suck'd thy fill.

—Where art thou gone my own dear child?

What wicked looks are those I see?

Alas! alas! that look so wild,

It never, never came from me:

If thou art mad, my pretty lad,

Then I must be for ever sad. 90

Oh! smile on me, my little lamb!

For I thy own dear mother am.

My love for thee has well been tried:

I've sought thy father far and wide.

I know the poisons of the shade,

I know the earth-nuts1 fit for food;

Then, pretty dear, be not afraid;

We'll find thy father in the wood.

Now laugh and be gay, to the woods away!

And there, my babe; we'll live for aye." 100

earth-nuts] The round tubers of umbelliferous plants, also called "earth-chestnuts" or "pig-nuts"; possibly recalling Caliban's speech in II.ii of Shakespeare's The Tempest: "I prithee, let me bring thee where crabs grow;/And I with my long nails will dig thee pignuts;/Show thee a jay's nest and instruct thee how/ To snare the nimble marmoset;"

THE IDIOT BOY

'Tis eight o'clock,—a clear March night, The moon is up—the sky is blue, The owlet in the moonlight air,

He shouts from nobody knows where;

He lengthens out his lonely shout,

Halloo! halloo! a long halloo!1

—Why bustle thus about your door,

What means this bustle, Betty Foy?

Why are you in this mighty fret?

And why on horseback have you set 10 Him whom you love, your idiot boy?

Beneath the moon that shines so bright,

Till she is tired, let Betty Foy

With girt2 and stirrup fiddle-faddle;3

But wherefore set upon a saddle

Him whom she loves, her idiot boy?

There's scarce a soul that's out of bed;

Good Betty! put him down again;

His lips with joy they burr at you,

But, Betty! what has he to do 20 With stirrup, saddle, or with rein?

The world will say 'tis very idle,

Bethink you of the time of night;

There's not a mother, no not one,

But when she hears what you have done,

Oh! Betty she'll be in a fright.

But Betty's bent on her intent,

For her good neighbour, Susan Gale,

Old Susan, she who dwells alone,

Is sick, and makes a piteous moan, 30 As if her very life would fail.

There's not a house within a mile,

No hand to help them in distress:

Old Susan lies a bed in pain,

And sorely puzzled are the twain,

For what she ails they cannot guess.

And Betty's husband's at the wood,

Where by the week he doth abide,

A woodman in the distant vale;

There's none to help poor Susan Gale, 40 What must be done? what will betide?

And Betty from the lane has fetched

Her pony, that is mild and good,

Whether he be in joy or pain,

Feeding at will along the lane,

Or bringing faggots from the wood.

And he is all in travelling trim,

And by the moonlight, Betty Foy

Has up upon the saddle set,

The like was never heard of yet, 50 Him whom she loves, her idiot boy.

And he must post without delay Across the bridge that's in the dale, And by the church, and o'er the down, To bring a doctor from the town, Or she will die, old Susan Gale.

'Tis ... halloo!] Recalling lines 1–5 of Coleridge's "Christabel." See Appendix B, p. 435.

girt] A saddle-girth, the leather strap which secures the saddle on the horse's back.

fiddle-faddle] To fuss over petty trifles.

1hurly-burly] Commotion or tumult.

There is no need of boot or spur,

There is no need of whip or wand,

For Johnny has his holly-bough,

And with a hurly-burly1 now 60 He shakes the green bough in his hand.

And Betty o'er and o'er has told

The boy who is her best delight,

Both what to follow, what to shun,

What do, and what to leave undone,

How turn to left, and how to right.

And Betty's most especial charge,

Was, "Johnny! Johnny! mind that you

Come home again, nor stop at all,

Come home again, whate'er befal, 70 My Johnny do, I pray you do."

To this did Johnny answer make,

Both with his head, and with his hand,

And proudly shook the bridle too,

And then! his words were not a few,

Which Betty well could understand.

And now that Johnny is just going,

Though Betty's in a mighty flurry,

She gently pats the pony's side,

On which her idiot boy must ride, 80 And seems no longer in a hurry.

But when the pony moved his legs,

Oh! then for the poor idiot boy!

For joy he cannot hold the bridle,

For joy his head and heels are idle,

He's idle all for very joy.

And while the pony moves his legs,

In Johnny's left-hand you may see,

The green bough's motionless and dead;

The moon that shines above his head 90 Is not more still and mute than he.

His heart it was so full of glee,

That till full fifty yards were gone,

He quite forgot his holly whip,

And all his skill in horsemanship,

Oh! happy, happy, happy John.

And Betty's standing at the door,

And Betty's face with joy o'erflows,

Proud of herself, and proud of him,

She sees him in his travelling trim; 100 How quietly her Johnny goes.

The silence of her idiot boy,

What hopes it sends to Betty's heart!

He's at the guide-post—he turns right,

She watches till he's out of sight,

And Betty will not then depart.

Burr, burr—now Johnny's lips they burr,1

As loud as any mill, or near it,

Meek as a lamb the pony moves,

And Johnny makes the noise he loves, 110 And Betty listens, glad to hear it.

Away she hies to Susan Gale:

And Johnny's in a merry tune,

The owlets hoot, the owlets curr,2

And Johnny's lips they burr, burr, burr,

And on he goes beneath the moon.

His steed and he right well agree,

For of this pony there's a rumour,

That should he lose his eyes and ears,

And should he live a thousand years, 120 He never will be out of humour.

But then he is a horse that thinks!

And when he thinks his pace is slack;

Now, though he knows poor Johnny well,

Yet for his life he cannot tell

What he has got upon his back.

So through the moonlight lanes they go,

And far into the moonlight dale,

And by the church, and o'er the down,

burr] To pronounce a strong uvular r (instead of a trilled r), done in England's northernmost counties; more generally, to speak indistinctly.

curr] To make a low murmuring sound, as with the cooing of a dove or the purring of a cat.

To bring a doctor from the town, 130

To comfort poor old Susan Gale.

And Betty, now at Susan's side,

Is in the middle of her story,

What comfort Johnny soon will bring,

With many a most diverting thing,

Of Johnny's wit and Johnny's glory.

And Betty's still at Susan's side:

By this time she's not quite so flurried;

Demure with porringer and plate

She sits, as if in Susan's fate 140

Her life and soul were buried.

But Betty, poor good woman! she,

You plainly in her face may read it,

Could lend out of that moment's store

Five years of happiness or more,

To any that might need it.

But yet I guess that now and then

With Betty all was not so well,

And to the road she turns her ears,

And thence full many a sound she hears,   150

Which she to Susan will not tell.

Poor Susan moans, poor Susan groans,

"As sure as there's a moon in heaven,"

Cries Betty, "he'll be back again;

They'll both be here, 'tis almost ten,

They'll both be here before eleven."

Poor Susan moans, poor Susan groans,

The clock gives warning for eleven;

'Tis on the stroke—"If Johnny's near,"

Quoth Betty "he will soon be here,   160

As sure as there's a moon in heaven."

The clock is on the stroke of twelve,

And Johnny is not yet in sight,

The moon's in heaven, as Betty sees,

But Betty is not quite at ease;

And Susan has a dreadful night.

And Betty, half an hour ago,

On Johnny vile reflections cast;

"A little idle sauntering thing!"

With other names, an endless string, 170 But now that time is gone and past.

And Betty's drooping at the heart,

That happy time all past and gone,

"How can it be he is so late?

The doctor he has made him wait,

Susan! they'll both be here anon."

And Susan's growing worse and worse,

And Betty's in a sad quandary;

And then there's nobody to say

If she must go or she must stay: 180 —She's in a sad quandary.

The clock is on the stroke of one;

But neither Doctor nor his guide

Appear along the moonlight road,

There's neither horse nor man abroad,

And Betty's still at Susan's side.

And Susan she begins to fear

Of sad mischances not a few,

That Johnny may perhaps be drown'd,

Or lost perhaps, and never found; 190 Which they must both for ever rue.

She prefaced half a hint of this

With, "God forbid it should be true!" At the first word that Susan said Cried Betty, rising from the bed, "Susan, I'd gladly stay with you.

I must be gone, I must away,

Consider, Johnny's but half-wise;

Susan, we must take care of him,

If he is hurt in life or limb"— 200 "Oh God forbid!" poor Susan cries.

"What can I do?" says Betty, going,

"What can I do to ease your pain?

Good Susan tell me, and I'll stay;

I fear you're in a dreadful way,

But I shall soon be back again."

"Good Betty go, good Betty go, There's nothing that can ease my pain." Then off she hies, but with a prayer

That God poor Susan's life would spare, 210 Till she comes back again.

So, through the moonlight lane she goes,

And far into the moonlight dale;

And how she ran, and how she walked,

And all that to herself she talked,

Would surely be a tedious tale.

In high and low, above, below,

In great and small, in round and square, In tree and tower was Johnny seen,

In bush and brake,1 in black and green, 220 'Twas Johnny, Johnny, every where.

She's past the bridge that's in the dale,

And now the thought torments her sore,

Johnny perhaps his horse forsook,

To hunt the moon that's in the brook,

And never will be heard of more.

And now she's high upon the down,

Alone amid a prospect wide;

There's neither Johnny nor his horse,

Among the fern or in the gorse;2 230 There's neither doctor nor his guide.

"Oh saints! what is become of him?

Perhaps he's climbed into an oak,

Where he will stay till he is dead;

Or sadly he has been misled,

And joined the wandering gypsey-folk.

Or him that wicked pony's carried

To the dark cave, the goblins' hall,

Or in the castle he's pursuing,

Among the ghosts, his own undoing; 240 Or playing with the waterfall."

At poor old Susan then she railed,

While to the town she posts away;

"If Susan had not been so ill,

Alas! I should have had him still,

My Johnny, till my dying day."

Poor Betty! in this sad distemper,

The doctor's self would hardly spare,

Unworthy things she talked and wild,

Even he, of cattle the most mild, 250 The pony had his share.

brake] Clump of bushes; a thicket.

gorse] Furze, a spiny evergreen shrub that grows in wastelands.

And now she's got into the town,

And to the doctor's door she hies;

'Tis silence all on every side;

The town so long, the town so wide, Is silent as the skies.

And now she's at the doctor's door,

She lifts the knocker, rap, rap, rap,

The doctor at the casement shews,

His glimmering eyes that peep and doze; 260 And one hand rubs his old night-cap.

"Oh Doctor! Doctor! where's my Johnny?" "I'm here, what is't you want with me?"
"Oh Sir! you know I'm Betty Foy, And I have lost my poor dear boy,

You know him—him you often see;

He's not so wise as some folks be," "The devil take his wisdom!" said The Doctor, looking somewhat grim,

"What, woman! should I know of him?" 270 And, grumbling, he went back to bed.

"O woe is me! O woe is me!

Here will I die; here will I die;

I thought to find my Johnny here,

But he is neither far nor near,

Oh! what a wretched mother I!"

She stops, she stands, she looks about,

Which way to turn she cannot tell.

Poor Betty! it would ease her pain

If she had heart to knock again; 280 —The clock strikes three—a dismal knell!1

Then up along the town she hies,

No wonder if her senses fail,

This piteous news so much it shock'd her,

She quite forgot to send the Doctor,

To comfort poor old Susan Gale.

And now she's high upon the down,

And she can see a mile of road,

"Oh cruel! I'm almost three-score;

Such night as this was ne'er before, 290 There's not a single soul abroad."

She listens, but she cannot hear

The foot of horse, the voice of man;

The streams with softest sound are flowing,

The grass you almost hear it growing,

You hear it now if e'er you can.

The owlets through the long blue night

Are shouting to each other still:

Fond lovers, yet not quite hob nob,2

They lengthen out the tremulous sob, 300 That echoes far from hill to hill.

Poor Betty now has lost all hope,

Her thoughts are bent on deadly sin;

A green-grown pond3 she just has pass'd,

knell] The sound of a bell rung slowly and solemnly, as immediately after a death or at a funeral.

hob nob] On familiar terms.

green-grown pond] Standing water covered with algae.

And from the brink she hurries fast, Lest she should drown herself therein.

And now she sits her down and weeps; Such tears she never shed before; "Oh dear, dear pony! my sweet joy!

Oh carry back my idiot boy! 310 And we will ne'er o'erload thee more."

A thought is come into her head;

"The pony he is mild and good,

And we have always used him well;

Perhaps he's gone along the dell,

And carried Johnny to the wood."

Then up she springs as if on wings;

She thinks no more of deadly sin;

If Betty fifty ponds should see,

The last of all her thoughts would be, 320 To drown herself therein.

Oh reader! now that I might tell

What Johnny and his horse are doing!

What they've been doing all this time,

Oh could I put it into rhyme,

A most delightful tale pursuing!

Perhaps, and no unlikely thought!

He with his pony now doth roam

The cliffs and peaks so high that are,

To lay his hands upon a star, 330 And in his pocket bring it home.

Perhaps he's turned himself about,

His face unto his horse's tail,

And still and mute, in wonder lost,

All like a silent horseman-ghost,

He travels on along the vale.

And now, perhaps, he's hunting sheep,

A fierce and dreadful hunter he!

Yon valley, that's so trim and green,

In five months' time, should he be seen, 340 A desert wilderness will be.

Perhaps, with head and heels on fire,

And like the very soul of evil,

He's galloping away, away,

And so he'll gallop on for aye,

The bane of all that dread the devil.1

I to the muses have been bound,

These fourteen years, by strong indentures; Oh gentle muses! let me tell

But half of what to him befel, 350 For sure he met with strange adventures.

Oh gentle muses! is this kind?

Why will ye thus my suit repel?

Why of your further aid bereave me?

And can you thus unfriended leave me?

Ye muses! whom I love so well.

Who's yon, that, near the waterfall,

Which thunders down with headlong force, Beneath the moon, yet shining fair,

As careless as if nothing were, 360 Sits upright on a feeding horse?

Unto his horse, that's feeding free,

He seems, I think, the rein to give;

Of moon or stars he takes no heed;

Of such we in romances read,

—'Tis Johnny! Johnny! as I live.

And that's the very pony too.

Where is she, where is Betty Foy?

She hardly can sustain her fears;

The roaring water-fall she hears, 370 And cannot find her idiot boy.

Your pony's worth his weight in gold,

Then calm your terrors, Betty Foy!

She's coming from among the trees,

And now, all full in view, she sees

Him whom she loves, her idiot boy.

Perhaps ... devil] Recalling lines 185–96 of "Lenora" by German poet Gottfried August Bürger. See Appendix G, p. 523.

And Betty sees the pony too: .

Why stand you thus Good Betty Foy?

It is no goblin, 'tis no ghost,

'Tis he whom you so long have lost,   380

He whom you love, your idiot boy.

She looks again—her arms are up—

She screams—she cannot move for joy;

She darts as with a torrent's force,

She has almost o'erturned the horse,

And fast she holds her idiot boy.

And Johnny burrs and laughs aloud,

Whether in cunning or in joy,

I cannot tell; but while he laughs,

Betty a drunken pleasure quaffs,   390

To hear again her idiot boy.

And now she's at the pony's tail,

And now she's at the pony's head,

On that side now, and now on this,

And almost stifled with her bliss,

A few sad tears does Betty shed.

She kisses o'er and o'er again,

Him whom she loves, her idiot boy,

She's happy here, she's happy there,

She is uneasy every where;   400

Her limbs are all alive with joy.

She pats the pony, where or when

She knows not, happy Betty Foy!

The little pony glad may be,

But he is milder far than she,

You hardly can perceive his joy.

"Oh! Johnny, never mind the Doctor;

You've done your best, and that is all."

She took the reins, when this was said,

And gently turned the pony's head   410

From the loud water-fall.

By this the stars were almost gone,

The moon was setting on the hill,

So pale you scarcely looked at her:

The little birds began to stir,

Though yet their tongues were still.

The pony, Betty, and her boy,

Wind slowly through the woody dale:

And who is she, be-times abroad,

That hobbles up the steep rough road? 420 Who is it, but old Susan Gale?

Long Susan lay deep lost in thought,

And many dreadful fears beset her,

Both for her messenger and nurse;

And as her mind grew worse and worse,

Her body it grew better.

She turned, she toss'd herself in bed,

On all sides doubts and terrors met her;

Point after point did she discuss;

And while her mind was fighting thus, 430 Her body still grew better.

"Alas! what is become of them?

These fears can never be endured,

I'll to the wood."—The word scarce said,

Did Susan rise up from her bed,

As if by magic cured.

Away she posts up hill and down,

And to the wood at length is come,

She spies her friends, she shouts a greeting;

Oh me! it is a merry meeting, 440 As ever was in Christendom.

The owls have hardly sung their last,

While our four travellers homeward wend;

The owls have hooted all night long,

And with the owls began my song,

And with the owls must end.

For while they all were travelling home,

Cried Betty, "Tell us Johnny, do,

Where all this long night you have been,

What you have heard, what you have seen,   450

And Johnny, mind you tell us true."

Now Johnny all night long had heard

The owls in tuneful concert strive;

No doubt too he the moon had seen;

For in the moonlight he had been

From eight o'clock till five.

And thus to Betty's question, he

Made answer, like a traveller bold,

(His very words I give to you,)

"The cocks did crow to-whoo, to-whoo,

And the sun did shine so cold."   460

—Thus answered Johnny in his glory,

And that was all his travel's story.

LINES WRITTEN NEAR RICHMOND, UPON THE THAMES,
AT EVENING1

How rich the wave, in front, imprest

With evening-twilight's summer hues,2

While, facing thus the crimson west,

The boat her silent path pursues!

And see how dark the backward stream!

A little moment past, so smiling!

And still, perhaps, with faithless gleam,

Some other loiterer beguiling.

Such views the youthful bard allure,

But, heedless of the following gloom, 10 He deems their colours shall endure 'Till peace go with him to the tomb.

—And let him nurse his fond deceit,

And what if he must die in sorrow!

Who would not cherish dreams so sweet, Though grief and pain may come to-morrow?

Glide gently, thus for ever glide,

O Thames! that other bards may see,

As lovely visions by thy side

As now, fair river! come to me. 20 Oh glide, fair stream! for ever so;3

By Wordsworth. Richmond is a suburb southwest of central London; see Appendix H, p. 542. In the 1800 edition, lines 1–16 become a separate poem, entitled "Lines Written when sailing in a Boat at Evening." The remaining stanzas appear as "Lines Written near Richmond upon the Thames." In 1802, both poems were moved to volume two, probably to make room for the expanded Preface.

How ... hues] In Robert Southey's presentation copy of the 1805 edition of Lyrical Ballads (British Library call number C.58.bb.23), lines 1–2 are altered (in what appears Southey's hand) to: "How richly glows the water's breast/Before us tinged with evening hues,"Oh glide ... ever so] Recalling the refrain that concludes each stanza of Edmund Spenser's Prothalamion (1596): "Sweete Themmes runne softly, till I end my Song."

Thy quiet soul on all bestowing,

'Till all our minds for ever flow,

As thy deep waters now are flowing.

Vain thought! yet be as now thou art,

That in thy waters may be seen

The image of a poet's heart,

How bright, how solemn, how serene!

Such heart did once the poet bless,

Who, pouring here a* later ditty,   30

Could find no refuge from distress,

But in the milder grief of pity.

Remembrance! as we glide along,

For him suspend the dashing oar,

And pray that never child of Song

May know his freezing sorrows more.1

How calm! how still! the only sound,

The dripping of the oar suspended!

—The evening darkness gathers round

By virtue's holiest powers attended.   40

EXPOSTULATION AND REPLY2

"Why, William, on that old grey stone, Thus for the length of half a day, Why, William, sit you thus alone, And dream your time away?

Where are your books? that light bequeath'd

To beings else forlorn and blind!

Up! Up! and drink the spirit breath'd

From dead men to their kind.

"You look round on your mother earth, As if she for no purpose bore you;

As if you were her first-born birth, And none had lived before you!"

One morning thus, by Esthwaite lake,

When life was sweet, I knew not why,

To me my good friend Matthew spake,

And thus I made reply.

"The eye it cannot chuse but see, We cannot bid the ear be still; Our bodies feel, where'er they be, Against, or with our will."

"Nor less I deem that there are powers Which of themselves our minds impress, That we can feed this mind of ours In a wise passiveness."

"Think you, mid all this mighty sum Of things for ever speaking,

That nothing of itself will come, But we must still be seeking?"

"—Then ask not wherefore, here, alone, Conversing as I may,

I sit upon this old grey stone,

And dream my time away."

Collins's Ode on the death of Thomson, the last written, I believe, of the poems which were published during his life-time. This Ode is also alluded to in the next stanza. [Wordsworth's note. Collins's "Ode" was published in 1749.]

Remembrance! ... more] Echoing lines 13–16 of Collins's "Ode": "Remembrance oft shall haunt the Shore/When Thames in Summer-wreaths is drest,/And oft suspend the dashing Oar/To bid his gentle Spirit rest!"

By Wordsworth.

THE TABLES TURNED;
AN EVENING SCENE, ON THE SAME SUBJECT1

Up! up! my friend, and clear your looks,

Why all this toil and trouble?

Up! up! my friend, and quit your books,

Or surely you'll grow double.

The sun, above the mountain's head,

A freshening lustre mellow

Through all the long green fields has spread,

His first sweet evening yellow.

Books! 'tis a dull and endless strife,

Come, hear the woodland linnet,   10

How sweet his music; on my life

There's more of wisdom in it.

And hark! how blithe the throstle2 sings!

And he is no mean preacher;

Come forth into the light of things,

Let Nature be your teacher.

She has a world of ready wealth,

Our minds and hearts to bless—

Spontaneous wisdom breathed by health,

Truth breathed by chearfulness.   20

One impulse from a vernal wood

May teach you more of man;

Of moral evil and of good,

Than all the sages can.

Sweet is the lore which nature brings; Our meddling intellect

Mishapes the beauteous forms of things; —We murder to dissect.

Enough of science and of art;

Close up these barren leaves; 30

Come forth, and bring with you a heart

That watches and receives.

By Wordsworth.

throstle] The thrush, a songbird common in Britain.

OLD MAN TRAVELLING;
ANIMAL TRANQUILLITY AND DECAY,
A SKETCH 1

The little hedge-row birds,

That peck along the road, regard him not.

He travels on, and in his face, his step,

His gait, is one expression; every limb,

His look and bending figure, all bespeak

A man who does not move with pain, but moves

With thought—He is insensibly subdued

To settled quiet: he is one by whom

All effort seems forgotten, one to whom

Long patience has such mild composure given,   10

That patience now doth seem a thing, of which

He hath no need. He is by nature led

To peace so perfect, that the young behold

With envy, what the old man hardly feels.

—I asked him whither he was bound, and what

The object of his journey; he replied

"Sir! I am going many miles to take

A last leave of my son, a mariner,

Who from a sea-fight has been brought to Falmouth,2

And there is dying in an hospital."3   20

By Wordsworth. 1800: the title is shortened to "Animal Tranquility and

Decay: A Sketch."

Falmouth] A port and shipbuilding center in the English county of Cornwall. See Appendix H, p. 542.

I asked him ... in a hospital] The 1800 edition removes the quotation marks from lines 17–20 so that they are spoken by the narrator; Wordsworth deleted lines 15–20 from the poem in 1815.

THE COMPLAINT OF A FORSAKEN
INDIAN WOMAN1

[When a Northern Indian, from sickness, is unable to continue his journey with his companions; he is left behind, covered over with Deer-skins, and is supplied with water, food, and fuel if the situa-tion of the place will afford it. He is informed of the track which his companions intend to pursue, and if he is unable to follow, or overtake them, he perishes alone in the Desart; unless he should have the good fortune to fall in with some other Tribes of Indians. It is unnecessary to add that the females are equally, or still more, exposed to the same fate. See that very interesting work, Hearne's Journey from Hudson's Bay to the Northern Ocean.2 When the Northern Lights, as the same writer informs us, vary their posi-tion in the air, they make a rustling and a crackling noise.This cir-cumstance is alluded to in the first stanza of the following poem.]

THE COMPLAINT, &c.

Before I see another day,

Oh let my body die away!

In sleep I heard the northern gleams;

The stars they were among my dreams;

In sleep did I behold the skies,

I saw the crackling flashes drive;

And yet they are upon my eyes,

And yet I am alive.

Before I see another day,

Oh let my body die away!   10

By Wordsworth. In 1802, Wordsworth moved this poem to volume two.

Hearne ... Ocean] Wordsworth refers to p. 203 of Samuel Hearne, A Journey from Prince of Wales's Fort in Hudson's Bay to the Northern Ocean

... 1769–1772 (1795): "The poor woman ... came up with us several times, after having been left in the manner described. At length, poor creature! she dropped behind, and no one attempted to go back in search of her."

My fire is dead: it knew no pain;

Yet is it dead, and I remain.

All stiff with ice the ashes lie;

And they are dead, and I will die.

When I was well, I wished to live,

For clothes, for warmth, for food, and fire;

But they to me no joy can give,

No pleasure now, and no desire.

Then here contented will I lie;

Alone I cannot fear to die. 20

Alas! you might have dragged me on

Another day, a single one!

Too soon despair o'er me prevailed;

Too soon my heartless spirit failed;1

When you were gone my limbs were stronger,

And Oh how grievously I rue,

That, afterwards, a little longer,

My friends, I did not follow you!

For strong and without pain I lay,

My friends, when you were gone away. 30

My child! they gave thee to another,

A woman who was not thy mother.

When from my arms my babe they took,

On me how strangely did he look!

Through his whole body something ran,

A most strange something did I see;

—As if he strove to be a man,

That he might pull the sledge for me.

And then he stretched his arms, how wild!

Oh mercy! like a little child.   40

My little joy! my little pride!

In two days more I must have died.

Then do not weep and grieve for me;

I feel I must have died with thee.

Oh wind that o'er my head art flying,

Too soon despair ... failed] In Robert Southey's presentation copy of the 1805 edition of Lyrical Ballads (British Library C.58.bb.23), lines 23–24 are altered (in what appears to be Southey's hand) to: "Too soon I yielded to despair/Why did ye listen to my prayer!"

The way my friends their course did bend,

I should not feel the pain of dying,

Could I with thee a message send.

Too soon, my friends, you went away;

For I had many things to say.   50

I'll follow you across the snow,

You travel heavily and slow:

In spite of all my weary pain,

I'll look upon your tents again.

My fire is dead, and snowy white

The water which beside it stood;

The wolf has come to me to-night,

And he has stolen away my food.

For ever left alone am I,

Then wherefore should I fear to die? 60

My journey will be shortly run,

I shall not see another sun,

I cannot lift my limbs to know

If they have any life or no.

My poor forsaken child! if I

For once could have thee close to me,

With happy heart I then would die,

And my last thoughts would happy be.

I feel my body die away,

I shall not see another day.1 70

THE CONVICT2

The glory of evening was spread through the west; —On the slope of a mountain I stood,

While the joy that precedes the calm season of rest Rang loud through the meadow and wood.

"And must we then part from a dwelling so fair?" In the pain of my spirit I said,

And with a deep sadness I turned, to repair To the cell where the convict is laid.

The thick-ribbed walls that o'ershadow the gate

Resound; and the dungeons unfold: 10

I pause; and at length, through the glimmering grate,

That outcast of pity behold.

His black matted head on his shoulder is bent,

And deep is the sigh of his breath,

And with stedfast dejection his eyes are intent

On the fetters that link him to death.

'Tis sorrow enough on that visage to gaze,

That body dismiss'd from his care;

Yet my fancy has pierced to his heart, and pourtrays

More terrible images there.   20

His bones are consumed, and his life-blood is dried, With wishes the past to undo;

And his crime, through the pains that o'erwhelm him, descried, Still blackens and grows on his view.

When from the dark synod,1 or blood-reeking field,

To his chamber the monarch is led,

All soothers of sense their soft virtue shall yield,

And quietness pillow his head.

But if grief, self-consumed, in oblivion would doze,

My journey ... another day] In Robert Southey's presentation copy of the 1805 edition of Lyrical Ballads (British Library C.58.bb.23), lines 61–70 are crossed out.

By Wordsworth. The poem was dropped from subsequent editions of Lyrical Ballads.

And conscience her tortures appease, 30 'Mid tumult and uproar this man must repose; In the comfortless vault of disease.

When his fetters at night have so press'd on his limbs,

That the weight can no longer be borne,

If, while a half-slumber his memory bedims,

The wretch on his pallet should turn,

While the jail-mastiff howls at the dull clanking chain,

From the roots of his hair there shall start

A thousand sharp punctures of cold-sweating pain,

And terror shall leap at his heart.   40

But now he half-raises his deep-sunken eye,

And the motion unsettles a tear;

The silence of sorrow it seems to supply,

And asks of me why I am here.

"Poor victim! no idle intruder has stood

With o'erweening complacence our state to compare,

But one, whose first wish is the wish to be good,

Is come as a brother thy sorrows to share.

At thy name though compassion her nature resign,

Though in virtue's proud mouth thy report be a stain,   50

My care, if the arm of the mighty were mine,

Would plant thee where yet thou might'st blossom again."1

1synod] An assembly or council

LINES

Written a few miles above TINTERN ABBEY, and revisiting the banks of the WYE during a Tour. July 13, 1798.

Five years have passed; five summers, with the length Of five long winters! and again I hear

These waters, rolling from their mountain-springs

With a sweet inland murmur. —Once again

Do I behold these steep and lofty cliffs,

Which on a wild secluded scene impress

Thoughts of more deep seclusion; and connect

The landscape with the quiet of the sky.

The day is come when I again repose Here, under this dark sycamore, and view

These plots of cottage-ground, these orchard-tufts,

Which, at this season, with their unripe fruits,

Among the woods and copses lose themselves,

Nor, with their green and simple hue, disturb

The wild green landscape. Once again I see

These hedge-rows, hardly hedge-rows, little lines

Of sportive wood run wild; these pastoral farms

Green to the very door; and wreathes of smoke

Sent up, in silence, from among the trees,

With some uncertain notice, as might seem,

Of vagrant dwellers in the houseless woods,

Or of some hermit's cave, where by his fire

The hermit sits alone.

Though absent long.

These forms of beauty have not been to me,

As is a landscape to a blind man's eye:

But oft, in lonely rooms, and mid the din

Of towns and cities, I have owed to them,

In hours of wariness, sensations sweet,

Felt in the blood, and felt along the heart,

And passing even into my purer mind,

With tranquil restoration:—feelings too

Of unremembered pleasure: such, perhaps,

As may have had no trivial influence

On that best portion of a good man's life;

His little, nameless, unremembered acts

Of kindness and of love. Nor less, I trust,

To them I may have owed another gift,

Of aspect more sublime; that blessed mood,

In which the burthen of the mystery,

In which the heavy and the weary weight Of all this unintelligible world

Is lighten'd:—that serene and blessed mood; In which the affections gently lead us on,

Until, the breath of this corporeal frame,

And even the motion of our human blood

Almost suspended, we are laid asleep

In body, and become a living soul:

While with an eye made quiet by the power

Of harmony, and the deep power of joy,

We see into the life of things.

If this

Be but a vain belief, yet, oh! how oft,

In darkness, and amid the many shapes

Of joyless day-light; when the fretful stir

Unprofitable, and the fever of the world,

Have hung upon the beatings of my heart,

How oft, in spirit, have I turned to thee

O sylvan Wye! Thou wanderer through the woods, How often has my spirit turned to thee!

And now, with gleams, of half-extinguish'd thought,

With many recognitions dim and faint,

And somewhat of a sad perplexity,

The picture of the mind revives again:

While here I stand, not only with the sense

Of present pleasure, but with pleasing thoughts

That in this moment there is life and food

For future years. And so I dare to hope

Though changed, no doubt, from what I was, when first

I came among these hills; when like a roe

I bounded o'er the mountains, by the sides

Of the deep rivers, and the lonely streams,

Wherever nature led: more like a man

Flying from something that he dreads, than one

Who sought the thing he loved. For nature then

(The coarser pleasures of my boyish days,

And their glad animal movements all gone by,)

To me was all in all.—I cannot paint

What then I was. The sounding cataract Haunted me like a passion: the tall rock,

The mountain, and the deep and gloomy wood,

Their colours and their forms, were then to me

An appetite: a feeling and a love,

That had no need of a remoter charm,

By thought supplied, or any interest

Unborrowed from the eye.—That time is past,

And all its aching joys are now no more,

And all its dizzy raptures. Not for this

Faint I, nor mourn nor murmur: other gifts

Have followed, for such loss, I would believe

Abundant recompence. For I have learned

To look on nature, not as in the hour

Of thoughtless youth, but hearing oftentimes The still, sad music of humanity,

Nor harsh nor grating, though of ample power To chasten and subdue. And I have felt

A presence that disturbs me with the joy

Of elevated thoughts; a sense sublime

Of something far more deeply interfused,

Whose dwelling is the light of setting suns,

And the round ocean, and the living air,

And the blue sky, and in the mind of man,

A motion and a spirit, that impels

All thinking things, all objects of all thought,

And rolls through all things. Therefore am I still

A lover of the meadows and the woods,

And mountains; and of all that we behold

From this green earth; of all the mighty world

Of eye and ear; both what they half create,

And what perceive; well pleased to recognize

In nature and the language of the sense,

The anchor of my purest thoughts, the nurse,

The guide, the guardian of my heart, and soul

Of all my moral being.

Nor, perchance,

If I were not thus taught, should I the more Suffer my genial spirits to decay?

For thou art with me, here, upon the banks Of this fair river; thou, my dearest Friend,

My dear, dear Friend, and in thy voice I catch

The language of my former heart, and read

My former pleasures in the shooting lights

Of thy wild eyes. Oh! yet a little while

May I behold in thee what I was once,

My dear, dear Sister! And this prayer I make,

Knowing that Nature never did betray

The heart that loved her; 'tis her privilege,

Through all the years of this our life, to lead

From joy to joy: for she can so inform

The mind that is within us, so impress

With quietness and beauty, and so feed

With lofty thoughts, that neither evil tongues,

Rash judgments, nor the sneers of selfish men,

Nor greetings where no kindness is, nor all

The dreary intercourse of daily life,

Shall e'er prevail against us, or disturb

Our chearful faith that all which we behold

Is full of blessings. Therefore let the moon

Shine on thee in thy solitary walk;

And let the misty mountain winds be free

To blow against thee: and in after years,

When these wild ecstasies shall be matured

Into a sober pleasure, when thy mind

Shall be a mansion for all lovely forms,

Thy memory be as a dwelling-place

For all sweet sounds and harmonies; Oh! then,

If solitude, or fear, or pain, or grief,

Should be thy portion, with what healing thoughts Of tender joy wilt thou remember me,

And these my exhortations! Nor perchance, If I should be, where I no more can hear

Thy voice, nor catch from thy wild eyes these gleams Of past existence, wilt thou then forget

That on the banks of this delightful stream

We stood together; and that I, so long

A worshipper of Nature, hither came,

Unwearied in that service: rather say

With warmer love, oh! with far deeper zeal

Of holier love. Nor wilt thou then forget,

That after many wanderings, many years

Of absence, these steep woods and lofty cliffs,

And this green pastoral landscape, were to me

More dear, both for themselves, and for thy sake.